Decoding Oral Language

European Monographs in Social Psychology

Series Editor HENRI TAJFEL

E. A. CARSWELL and R. ROMMETVEIT
Social Contexts of Messages, 1971

J. ISRAEL and H. TAJFEL
The Context of Social Psychology: A Critical Assessment, 1972

J. R. EISER and W. STROEBE
Categorization and Social Judgement, 1972

M. VON CRANACH and I. VINE
Social Communication and Movement, 1973

C. HERZLICH
Health and Illness: A Social Psychological Analysis, 1973

J. M. NUTTIN, JR. (and Annie Beckers)
The Illusion of Attitude Change: Towards a response contagion theory of
   persuasion, 1975

H. GILES and P. F. POWESLAND
Speech Style and Social Evaluation, 1975

J. CHADWICK-JONES
Social Exchange Theory: It's structure and influence in social psychology, 1976

M. BILLIG
Social Psychology and Intergroup Relations, 1976

S. MOSCOVICI
Social Influence and Social Change, 1976

R. SANDELL
Linguistic Style and Persuasion, 1977

H. GILES (Ed.)
Language, Ethnicity and Intergroup Relations, 1977

In preparation

H. TAJFEL (Ed.)
Differentiation between Social Groups: Studies in the social psychology of
   intergroup relations

EUROPEAN MONOGRAPHS IN SOCIAL PSYCHOLOGY 12
Series Editor: HENRI TAJFEL

Decoding Oral Language

ASTRI HEEN WOLD

Institute of Psychology, University of Oslo, Norway

1978

Published in cooperation with
EUROPEAN ASSOCIATION OF EXPERIMENTAL
SOCIAL PSYCHOLOGY
by
ACADEMIC PRESS *London, New York and San Francisco*
A Subsidiary of Harcourt Brace Jovanovich, Publishers

ACADEMIC PRESS INC. (LONDON) LTD.
24/28 Oval Road
London NW1

United States Edition published by
ACADEMIC PRESS INC.
111 Fifth Avenue
New York, New York 10003

Library of Congress Catalog Card Number: 77 76678
ISBN 0 12 336250 4

Typeset by Gloucester Typesetting Co. Ltd.
Printed in England by
Whitstable Litho Ltd.
Whitstable, Kent

Preface

Research is not, and should not be, a totally individual affair, and I have had the very great fortune to be part of a group of people around Ragnar Rommetveit, profoundly engaged in problems of language and communication. First of all I want to thank Ragnar Rommetveit for numerous significant discussions and warm and sincere interest and support.

During every phase of this work, I have also had the opportunity to discuss all kinds of problems with Rolv Mikkel Blakar. This has been most stimulating and many a time made me return to the work with renewed interest and courage. For this I want to thank him. The cooperation with Ragnar Rommetveit and Rolv Mikkel Blakar has rendered my research both more stimulating and meaningful to me.

Various subparts of this monograph have in earlier drafts been discussed in research seminars at the University of Oslo. I highly appreciate such opportunities which have given me insight and a lot of ideas, and I wish to express my gratitude towards each of the participants. Tore Helstrup and Karl Halvor Teigen have also read earlier drafts and they both deserve thanks for valuable comments.

For the statistical analysis of the data Thorleif Lund and Hans Magne Eikeland have been of great help. I want to thank them both and also the Computer-service for all kind assistance.

I also feel grateful towards Gunn Skartland Scheen for conscientious and good help in parts of the experimental work and to the subjects taking part in it.

The experimental investigations have been supported by funds from the Norwegian Research Council for Science and Humanities.

June, 1977.   ASTRI HEEN WOLD

Foreword

Some of the central issues in this book were raised and explored in a preliminary fashion in the very first monograph in this series. Astri Heen Wold was one of the young European contributors to that monograph, and their joint research ventures into extra- and intralinguistic context in verbal communication were at that time in some respects pioneering studies. They grew out of discontent with formally impressive yet sterile psycholinguistic research on "utterances *in vacuo*" and of an urge to know more about how words are imbued with meaning from other words and from the more inclusive pattern of social interaction in which verbal message transmission is embedded.

The author of this book pursues these issues further via conceptual analysis, in careful re-examination of previous social psychological and psycholinguistic research, and in a series of experiments of her own. Her aim is a dual one in the sense that she explicitly tries to interpret *individual cognitive strategies* in the light of genuinely *social psychological aspects of message transmission*. Oral discourse is social interaction extending over real time, and what is conveyed by any particular segment of such discourse is contingent upon what at that stage is taken for granted as a shared social reality. Comprehension, however, is in part a matter of integration of temporally chained components of information and hence contingent upon the individual listener's short term memory and mastery of word meaning. Decoding of oral language must therefore be examined as individual processing embedded in a genuinely social contexts of message transmission.

Astri Heen Wold's inquiries represent, because of this dual commitment, significant steps forward in our attempts to make the riddles of verbal communication intelligible in terms of general cognitive and social psychological theory.

RAGNAR ROMMETVEIT

Blommenholm
September, 1977

Contents

1

Introduction

The absolute reality of *time* is a central theme in the philosophy of Bergson. The conceptual intelligence, however, has a tendency to *spatialize* and *detemporalize* events. (Barrett, 1962; Bergson, 1962) Bergson has explicitly discussed the manifestation of these tendencies in the development of the physical sciences, and Goldman-Eisler (1968) maintains that the same tendencies appeared when psychology was developed in the direction of experimentation and quantification. This development resulted in (*ibid.* p. 2):

> time giving place to space and in simultaneity taking over from duration; science having eliminated from its calculation the temporal element and substituted homogeneity, repetition and simultaneity for heterogenity, continuity and succession.

Definite symptoms of detemporalization and spatialization may be found in studies of language and psycholinguistics influenced by Chomsky (Rommetveit, 1974). Arguments in support of such a claim are given in Part I in this monograph. Here we only want to note that the interest in deep-structure and surface-structure, which are a-temporal structures, the suggestion that meaning can be explicated by resort to propositions, as well as the concept of word meaning adopted, warrant the conclusion that language is detemporalized in Chomskian psycholinguistics.

In order to fully understand language from a psychological point of view, however, it seems necessary to take into consideration its temporal dimension. Language and communication take place in real time, and the structure of language is to a great extent given in temporal patterns because of the primary oral character of natural language. These aspects alone make it reasonable to direct attention towards the dimension of time. The neglect of this dimension in the important writings by Chomsky gives additional reason to focus this dimension. A general aim of this work is thus to explore some problems of language that are intimately related to its temporal aspects.

More specifically, the issues to be discussed could be characterized as problems concerning *temporal sequence of information.* The latter necessarily attract attention when language is considered with due attention towards its dimension of time. Why is one specific sequence chosen by the sender of a message, and how do alternative sequences affect the receiver? Such problems are explored both theoretically (Part I) and experimentally (Part II) in this monograph. The attention is in particular directed towards the latter part of the question. The two parts, however, should not be considered as independent. The attention towards time, change and development, furthermore, has made it reasonable primarily to explore *the processing* of the information as such rather than the output of processing.

Oral language is in the focus in this work. But in order to gain a broader perspective on sequence problems comparisons with written language and with the painting and understanding of pictures will be attempted.

The questions indicated above are only a few out of a greater set of problems that become important as soon as the consequences of the temporal dimension of language are considered. Other problems relate to experienced duration (Ornstein, 1969), to perception of sequences (e.g. Bakker, 1972), and to attempts to describe the time pattern of conversations (Goldman-Eisler, 1968). Such problems will not be discussed in this book, however.

The present work can be characterized by its attempt to combine a *social-psychological* and an *individual-processing* perspective on language problems. Language is primarily used for communication, and a proper understanding of language requires an understanding of how it is used as a mean to make something shared between sender and receiver. An explicit social-psychological approach to language is adopted by Ragnar Rommetveit (1972a, b, c, 1974) and the present work is clearly influenced by his discussions of language.

The communication perspective implies that we have to consider definite *constraints* both with respect to the ways in which an individual expresses himself and also to how he interprets the information he receives. When we talk, it makes a difference *to whom* we are talking. We choose our words in such a way that we expect the receiver to be able to understand. And conversely, when we are the receivers, we normally try to understand what the sender actually intended to convey. Thus, we do not feel free to process the information in whatever direction we want among all those opened up by the words in isolation. The aim of communication thus serves to constrain and also direct language processing, but the information has nevertheless to be processed by individuals. It is influenced by capacity limitations of the individual as well as by more specific individual strategies.

It is thus necessary to adopt a social perspective when language is to be understood. But when the aim is to explore in more detail what happens in a communication situation, this perspective must be supplemented with serious concern of individual processing. Although no attempt has been made to keep the perspectives strictly apart, the different sections of the book will reflect these perspectives to different degrees. The social-psychological perspective influence in particular Part I and Chapter 9 of Part II, whereas the individual-processing perspective has influenced the remaining parts of Part II to a great extent.

The present work should be read with these considerations in mind. Language as a social phenomenon constitutes in one way the general frame for the presentation, but it is also the author's aim to push the problems in an individual-processing direction. Concretely, the latter aim is pursued primarily by emphasis upon *memory processes.*

Issues concerning language and issues concerning memory have been discussed with rather few attempts towards cross-references (Fillenbaum, 1971, 1973). Fortunately, this tendency to isolate related fields seems to have changed in recent days, and even while I have been engaged in work on this book. Kintsch (1974) and Herriot (1974), among others, represent attempts to explore relationships between memory and language. Although the focus of main interest as well as the approach to language may vary, the present work shares their joint concern with language and memory processes. When this is said, however, it should be added that an understanding of language use is the primary interest and that data on recall performance are taken into consideration only to the extent that they seem relevant for language processing.

The experimental set-up used to explore sequence problems is one of *impression formation and recall.* Explorations of effects of alternative order of information have been a main and recurrent theme within the impression formation tradition (e.g. Asch, 1946; Anderson and Barrios, 1961; Anderson and Hubert, 1963; Luchins, 1966a, b; Anderson, 1968;

Margulis, Costanzo and Klein, 1971). The present experiments represent from one point of view an attempt to relate studies from this tradition more closely to the psychology of language. But again, impression
formation tasks are primarily used because they open up for explorations of language processing, not because of primary interest in this area
as such.

PART I

2

The Dimension of Time in Oral Language

In this part the generality of the dimension of time is emphasized. Attention towards the time dimension will necessarily spread to problems of sequence, and such problems are discussed at some length. The aim is primarily to relate the sequence problems encountered in oral language to sequence problems within other areas, mainly exemplified through written language and visual perception, in such a way that the special character of sequence problems in oral language becomes apparent.

In the last paragraphs, the claim that the time dimension has gained too little attention in recent work on language will be defended. This will be done mainly through an attempt to understand how the dimension of time is tackled within the dominant Harvard–M.I.T. linguistic and psycholinguistic tradition.

2.1. The generality of the time dimension

In the introduction it was maintained that the dimension of time was not given due attention in much recent work on language and communication. The dimension of time is crucial for the understanding of other sorts of activities as well. Its importance may even be more general than often considered. Thus Lenneberg maintains about *perception* (1967, p. 108):

> When we talk about visual patterns we consider only spatial dimensions, disregarding the dimension of time. Under most circumstances, time does seem to be irrelevant. Yet, physiological processes do have a temporal dimension, and even in the process of seeing, which strikes us as taking

place instantaneously, time plays a role. The identification of such simple figures as triangles and circles requires time and consequently, requires temporal integration in the central nervous system.

The importance of the dimension of time in perception is also emphasized by Neisser (1966, p. 41):

> There are no instantaneous perceptions, no unmediated glances into reality. The only way to use the term "perception" sensibly is in relation to the extended processes that can go on as long as the icon[1] continues.

and (*ibid.* p. 10):

> The central assertion is that seeing, hearing and remembering are all acts of *construction*, which may make more or less use of stimulus information depending on circumstances. The constructive processes are assumed to have two stages, of which the first is fast, crude, wholistic, and parallel while the second is deliberate, attentive, detailed and sequential.

When the time dimension of activities is brought into focus, this may have different implications. One may be an emphasis on problems connected with the sequence of elements "because any order or sequence temporarily unfolds itself", to borrow the words of Collaizzi (1971, p. 122). The present problem may be conceived of as one of such a class of sequence problems in that effects of alternative sequences of words are explored.

What is said above might conceal the similarity between the time problems conceived of as problems of sequence and some other problems related to time. In many cases it is rather easy to conceive of activities as existing of elements. Speech, for example, may be divided into the traditional elements of phonemes, morphemes, words, and sentences, and attention may be directed towards the specific sequence in which these elements are given. Other activities, however, may be more difficult to divide into elements. The process of understanding language, for example, is much more difficult to view in terms of sequences of discrete elements, probably because what happens at each moment is too confounded and complicated. But the process of understanding language can certainly be seen in its time dimension, with particular attention towards development over time. The commonality, the basis in the dimension of time is what is of importance in this connection. In the experiments to be reported in the second part of this monograph the dimension of time is attended to in two ways:

1. Icon is explained on p. 9.

a) The stimulus material is systematically varied with respect to temporal sequence.

(b) The aim is first of all to explore *the process of understanding language* as something developing over time rather than the final product of such a process.

2.2. Some problems related to sequence

A considerable number of psychological problems may be considered problems of *order* or *sequencing of elements*. Lashley (1951) has in his article "The problem of serial order in behavior" discussed such problems. He asks, for example, how it is possible to understand the processes which control the rapid successions of movements required to perform different motor skills (violin playing, typewriting) and how it is possible for a speaker to utter words in such an order as to form syntactically correct sentences. These problems all pertain to output or motor aspects of behavior. Problems of order, however, are relevant in relation to input aspects as well.

Sequence problems in visual perception can be illustrated by some experiments by Sperling (1960). He exposed different arrays of letters, for example:

TDR
SRN
FZR

to subjects for 50 msec by use of a tachistoscope, and asked them to report these letters afterwards. In some of his experiments his subjects were required to give a "whole" report, that is, to try to report all the letters. There were, however, more letters than the subjects could report correctly.

In other experiments Sperling used what was called a "partial" report. The subjects were in such cases asked to report on a special part of the array of letters by a signal which was given immediately *after* the display had been turned off. This special subset would then be reported extremely well. This can be explained by assuming that the visual input is in some way briefly stored after the display is turned off, and that the subjects can still "read" the arrays as if the stimulus were still active. This brief storage is what is called "icon" by Neisser.

The results of Sperling's experiments demonstrate *the importance of the sequence of information intake* (or more correctly, the importance of th sequence in which material stored in the icon is further processed). Only those letters first attended to can be reported later on.

The evidence comes from a highly artificial situation, but similar effects may be displayed in particular real-life situations where things happen at high speed. In cases of accidents, for example, different people may perceive what happens in different ways, some people noticing details or aspects of events which were not at all seen by others. This might even be the case when they all were looking rather directly at what happened. Such differences can perhaps in part be explained by different sequences of information intake.

The sequence of information intake may then be important when things happen rapidly, but it may also play a role when material is presented for a longer time. When subjects are presented with complex pictures, photographs of the fixation points of their eyes show that these may move across the picture in different ways (Kolers, 1973). What sort of consequences are then connected with a specific sequence of information intake? Most probably, the differences in perception due to different sequences would not be so great as in the experiment by Sperling or in case of some accidents where only the first elements attended to can be reported later on. It is still very probable, however, that different sequences of eye movements across a picture give rise to somewhat different impressions.

In connection with the examples above we may also explore other problems of order: What sort of factors determine the sequence of information intake? In the experiments by Sperling it was to a great extent controlled by the experimenter, but less is known about the determination of order in the other cases.

For an interesting discussion of some factors influencing the sequence of information intake from pictures, however, Kolers (*ibid.*) should be consulted.

Problems of order are thus encountered in many different areas of psychology. They seem to be of particular significance in the psychology of language, however. One of the most essential features of language is its pattern or structure, and Lenneberg (1967, p. 218) maintains that "the dimensions of language patterns are entirely of a temporal nature". The importance assigned by Lenneberg to the dimension of time in language is also revealed in his approach to aphasia. He tries to understand the diversity of aphasic symptoms as different kinds of temporal

disorders (*ibid.* p. 218–219). In an article emphasizing the importance
of identification of time relationship between events, Efron (1963) also
suggests that disorders of central mechanisms for sequence analysis
might be responsible for certain symptoms of aphasia.

The extensive exploitation of temporal patterns in language is given
by the very nature of the natural medium for language sounds. Use of
the vocal-auditory channel is one of the universal design-features of
language (Hockett, 1963). This means that all linguistic signals are
evanescent; they are rapidly fading away. Rapid fading is certainly a
characteristic of oral language. Written language, on the other hand, is
characterized by a relative permanence. Written manifestations, however, are secondary to, i.e. dependent upon and derived from, oral
language. The graphemes in our written medium, for instance, correspond roughly to the phonemes in the oral medium. The pattern or
structure which is mediated by temporal factors in oral language is
transformed into the spatial order of graphemes in written language.
The characteristics of sound and oral language have thus determined
what sort of spatial and visual factors are involved in many forms of
written language. In spite of this, the difference with respect to medium
also makes for different strategies of encoding and decoding. To such
differences we shall return.

In the above comments only phonemic forms of written language
systems have been kept in mind. The relationship between the two
media will be different when other systems of written language such as,
e.g. the pictorial form found in China, are considered. Such problems,
however, will not be discussed in this monograph.

Although the dimension of time clearly is very important for language, a categorical statement such as that "the dimensions of language
patterns are entirely of a temporal nature" (Lenneberg, 1967, p. 218)
may be questioned. Before proceeding to problems of temporal sequence,
some problems concerning structures or patterns which are not strictly
temporal, will therefore be mentioned.

Jakobson (1971) conceives of the phoneme as a bundle of simultaneously produced distinctive features. In a discussion of the funda-
mental character of the operations of combination and selection in
language, he argues against the exclusively linear character of language
(p. 74):

> The fundamental role which these two operations play in language was
> clearly realized by Ferdinand de Saussure. Yet of the two varieties of

combination—concurrence and concatenation—it was only the latter, the temporal sequence, which was recognized by the Geneva linguist. Despite his own insight into the phoneme as a set of distinctive features (elements différentiales des phonemes), the scholar succumbed to the traditional belief in the linear character of language "qui exclut la possibilité de prononcer deux elements a la fois".

Prosodic features of language may provide other examples of contemporal patterns. Prosodic features as such are clearly temporal, as the ordering of the words is temporal. But although the words are "carrying" the prosodic features, word order and prosodic features may vary independently of each other. It is possible to say the same sentence with different prosodic features as well as to use the same prosody on different sequences of words. As the way the sentence is understood is dependent both on the special way in which the words are said and on the special words themselves, this understanding seems to me to involve mechanisms of organization in addition to the purely temporal one.

Another point of importance is that language cannot be understood independent of the situation in which it occurs (Rommetveit, 1968, 1972b, c, 1974). The message conveyed by a sentence is dependent on the situation in which it is embedded. In order to master language in action, it is necessary to take into consideration the particular configuration of what is said and the situation in which it is uttered. This, again, points to the importance of simultaneous structures.

It is in this connection also tempting to bring in some considerations from the sign language of the deaf.[1] Van Mierlo (1968, p. 535) maintains that it is reasonable to talk about a "principe vertical" in addition to the "principe linéair" in such a case:

> It occurs, for instance, that deaf children make several signs at the same moment. *De Saussure's* "principe linéair" is accomplished by a "principe vertical" in this communication behavior.

As already mentioned, however, the above is not meant to deny the great importance of temporal patterns within the psychology of language. The comments are only meant to bring into focus patterns or structures of a simultaneous character as well, and thereby question Lenneberg's categorical formulation.

---

1. The question if and in what sense it is reasonable to consider the sign language of the deaf as language will not be taken up in this connection.

In connection with the discussion of sequence problems in visual perception, only input aspects were considered. Problems related to production or output, however, may also be attended to when the stimulus material is man-made, as was the case in the experiments by Sperling and the example of picture. When we turn to language, we have to attend both to "output" and "input". Every act of oral verbal communication involves both a speaker and a listener. The basic complementarity between the speaker and the listener, the I–you axis of communication, is strongly emphasized by Rommetveit (1972c, 1974). Because this complementarity may be reflected in sequence problems as well, some specific aspects of it will first be briefly discussed.

The complementarity between speaker and listener is revealed in encoding as well as decoding. According to Rommetveit, encoding involves an aspect of anticipatory decoding. This may be illustrated by the following examples:

(a) When I have invited American guests, and my children who do not understand English, are also present, I spontaneously change language code depending on to whom I am speaking at each moment.
(b) When I talk to my children, I most probably use a more restricted vocabulary than when discussing with adults.
(c) Similarly, when I talk to my friends and relatives, I try *not* to use the psychological terminology which I spontaneously adopt in discussion with other psychologists.

When it comes to decoding, we ordinarily understand on the premises of the speaker. This may also be illustrated by some examples:

(a) If the utterance includes deictic words, we immediately connect them to aspects of the outer situation or our prior conversation in the way presupposed by the speaker. If HE is used, we cannot tie the pronoun to any man that comes into our mind or happens to be in front of us. In order to understand the utterance, such a word must be interpreted as intended by the speaker.
(b) When a little girl who has just started to learn words referring to time such as YESTERDAY and TOMORROW tells me that she went on a trip with her mother yesterday, I would most probably *not* interpret YESTERDAY as referring exactly to the day before. It conveys to me that something has already happened, but does

not inform me exactly when this happened. When, on the other hand, some adult woman tells me that she went on a trip with her mother yesterday, I interpret this as exact information about time.

What is said above, however, must not be taken to mean that we always *manage to formulate* our utterance in such a way that we are understood, or that we always *manage to understand* the message the speaker tries to convey. The point is only that anticipatory decoding and understanding on the premises of the speaker are involved in ordinary communication situations, sometimes successfully, sometimes not. It seems therefore important to keep both poles, both the speaker and the listener in mind when we explore sequence problems in language.

The starting point for such explorations may be rather simple. Imagine a speaker who is going to describe something which is "out there", accessible to him experientially. As soon as he wants to say something more complicated than what may be conveyed by one word, sequence problems are encountered: It is simply impossible to utter more than one word at a time.

The speaker wants, for example, to describe a secretary he experiences as severe, cool and extraordinary. The secretary exists out there with all her characteristics *simultaneously*, whereas order of the words is neither *a priori* given nor automatically controlled by what is to be described. In this specific example, the speaker has a number of options. First, he has to choose between different syntactic forms. It is possible to say: A SECRETARY WHO IS SEVERE, COOL, AND EXTRAORDINARY or A SEVERE, COOL, AND EXTRAORDINARY SECRETARY. These forms seem to mediate essentially the same information. The choice of one particular syntactic form still leaves the speaker with additional options, however. It is possible to say: A SECRETARY WHO IS EXTRAORDINARY, COOL, AND SEVERE instead of A SECRETARY WHO IS SEVERE, COOL, AND EXTRAORDINARY, as above. How, then, is order to be determined?

Such a question could be approached at different levels. Interpreted in one particular way, this is Lashley's (1951) problem: It is legitimate to say A SECRETARY WHO IS SEVERE, COOL AND EXTRAORDINARY, but not A WHO SECRETARY SEVERE IS EXTRAORDINARY COOL. What sort of process makes it possible to utter words in a *sequence which is acceptable from a syntactic point of view*? This problem will not be given more attention here, however, because it is peripheral to the theme of main interest. The issue to be discussed will be choice *between alternative optional word orders each of which conforms to some acceptable syntactic form.* Why, then, is one particular sequence chosen at the expense of all other possibilities?

Relevant to this point is the existence of less strict "rules". Different authors have claimed that there may be constraints, for example, in the freedom to order adjectives (Vendler, 1963; Brown, 1965, p. 282; Martin, 1969). Such "rules" may describe highly frequent and preferred order of types of adjectives, and are thus of importance for an understanding of choice of order.

It is here presupposed, however, that these "rules" are not obligatory. Different sequences would most probably be accepted as grammatically correct by naive subject (cf. Appendix B). Thus, in spite of constraints, the speaker is still left options in such cases, and an exploration of factors that may influence choice at this level is here of primary interest.

If encoding involves aspects of anticipatory decoding, the latter may also affect the speaker's choice of the *word order.* This might be the case whenever word order as such has an impact upon the decoding process. An important point in this connection is that the rapid fading of sounds provides the speaker with *control of the sequence in which the words are perceived*: They must be perceived in exactly the same sequence as that in which they were produced. Because of the rapid fading of sounds and anticipatory decoding then, the speaker's intuitive or reflective knowledge of the *effect* of different word orders upon the listener might influence his choice. *Word order in encoding should hence be examined in close relationship to consequences of different word orders upon decoding.* Such consequences are explored in the experimental part of the present monograph. At this point possible consequences for retroactive processes, memory processes, and primacy/recency effects will therefore only be rather briefly discussed.

Attention mechanisms are relevant in this connection. The listener may be inattentive to parts of an utterance and thereby also "control" aspects of information intake. He may, however, only leave out parts of the information, he cannot change its order, and attention will therefore be disregarded in this discussion.

Thus, we continue to maintain that the words must be perceived in exactly the same sequence as that in which they were produced. This does not imply, however, that the decoding process has to be conceived of as consisting of "clicks of comprehension" accompanying each word —to use Roger Brown's (1958) illustrating terminology. Considerations concerning retroactive processes (Rommetveit, 1968, 1972c, 1974; Kvale, 1974a) and coding stations (Miller, 1956, 1962a; Rommetveit and Turner, 1967; Rommetveit, 1968; Blakar, 1970) are clearly relevant to an understanding of the decoding process. The extent to which retroactive processing is required, however, seems to be dependent upon sequence. The example of the secretary may again be used to illustrate this point.

As mentioned above, it is possible to describe the secretary in one of the following ways:

1. A SEVERE, COOL, AND EXTRAORDINARY SECRETARY
2. A SECRETARY WHO IS SEVERE, COOL, AND EXTRA-ORDINARY

If form 1 is used, retroactive processes will most probably constitute part of the decoding process, whereas this will not be the case if form 2 is chosen. When only A SEVERE, COOL . . . is heard, it is impossible for the listener to know what sort of entity is to be described. It might as well be, e.g. the weather or some style of architecture as a person. The meaning of SEVERE and COOL will be somewhat different in the three cases, and final decoding of adjectives has therefore to be postponed until the noun is heard. Decoding of the noun has then an effect on the final processing of preceding words, that is, a retroactive effect.

Lashley (1951, p. 120) gives the following example of a sentence requiring retroactive processing:

RAPID RIGHTING WITH HIS UNINJURED HAND SAVED FROM LOSS THE CONTENTS OF THE CAPSIZED CANOE.

In this sentence, when it is only heard, RIGHTING clearly is ambiguous. According to Lashley it takes at least 3 to 5 seconds from when the word is heard until "the associations which give meaning to righting are activated".

When discussing retroactive processes and postponement of final decoding, we should also keep in mind that we try to understand what is said on the premises of the speaker. When some parts of an utterance are known already, but essential information for final decoding still seems to be lacking, the listener may try to understand the first part as best he can, and he may create contexts or fill in the missing information himself. The obligation to understand on the premises of the speaker, however, works against such strategies: The aim of the listener is not only to understand *something*, it is to understand just *that which the listener wants to convey*. Such factors strengthen the influence of the speaker on the decoding process.

Constructions requiring retroactive processes often seem to put a heavy load on memory. In A SEVERE, COOL AND EXTRAORDINARY SECRETARY the listener has to keep in mind SEVERE, COOL and EXTRAORDINARY in one way or another until SECRETARY is heard. It may be easy in this example, but it is clearly possible to increase the number of adjectives and thus also the memory burden.

One special type of sentence seems to impose particularly heavy strains on memory capacities, namely the self-embedding sentence. Miller (1962b) gives the following example:

THE RACE THAT THE CAR THAT THE PEOPLE WHOM THE OBVIOUSLY NOT VERY WELL DRESSED MAN CALLED SOLD WON WAS HELD LAST SUMMER.

This sentence is, according to certain criteria, perfectly grammatical, but it is certainly difficult to understand (Miller, *ibid.*).[1] It can be transformed into what is called a right-recursive sentence, however:

THE OBVIOUSLY NOT VERY WELL DRESSED MAN CALLED THE PEOPLE WHO SOLD THE CAR THAT WON THE RACE THAT WAS HELD LAST SUMMER.

Thus, by choice among different syntactic forms, the speaker may also affect the ways and the extent to which memory processes become involved in decoding.[2]

Choice of sequence of adjectives also has consequences. Studies of impression formation have been interpreted as showing that the words *first heard* tend to be given more importance than words presented later (Asch, 1946, see also p. 59).

1. Cf. Chomsky's discussion of the difference between "grammatical" and "acceptable" (Chomsky, 1965, pp. 10–15).
2. Relationship between syntactic form and memory processing, moreover, have been experimentally explored in connection with the "depth" hypothesis by Yngve (1960). According to a review by Fillenbaum (1971, pp. 277–278), however, the results are from such a point of view inconsistent and difficult to interpret.

The sequence of production by the *speaker*, then, is clearly of importance for the *listener*. In view of what has been said about anticipatory decoding, moreover, we may also expect that *intuitive or reflective knowledge of effects of word order may influence choice of order*. We may ask if it is reasonable to expect that an ordinary speaker has any knowledge of such effects of order as those mentioned above. Within the conceptual framework of Rommetveit, with its emphasis on communication as a complementary process, this becomes an important question. Little is at present known about such matters, but they would deserve experimental exploration. First of all, the ordinary, naive, speaker may actually have some vague knowledge of the effect of different word orders. He most probably does not know that one syntactic form provides for more retroactive processes than another, or that one particular sequence puts more heavy load on memory processes than another, but he may know intuitively that some constructions are more complicated than others. Some of the results of Broen (1972), comparing the speech style of mothers talking to their young children, to their older children, and to other adults, provide some evidence of this point.

In connection with problems of primacy/recency related to the order of the adjectives, a preliminary experiment was performed by the author and a group of students. The subjects were given a noun and a set of adjectives and asked to arrange the adjectives in the order providing the most positive (or the most negative) impression of what was described. The results suggested that the speaker actually tends to arrange the words in such an order that the effect on the listener will be as he wishes. In this very preliminary exploration, then, the speaker demonstrated knowledge of order effects in the sense that he monitored sequence in accordance with desired outcomes.

Order effects in oral language have now primarily been discussed from the point of departure of "the ordinary speaker in ordinary situations". Most probably, however, some communication situations would profit more than others from the speaker's intuitive (or better: reflective) knowledge of order effects. Thus, if our task were to test a mentally retarded child with severe language problems, careful planning of the sequencing of words in the instruction might be of great importance. One legitimate sequence might result in failure on a specific task, while some alternative sequence might lead to success. To such problems we shall return at the end of the monograph (p. 180).

In the discussion above, the point of departure was sequence problems encountered whenever some reality "out there" is to be described so that another person gets to know about it. But this represents only one category of communication situations. Very often we want to inform others about what we ordinarily would call our "thoughts", and problems become much more difficult as soon as "thoughts" are brought into the discussion. The relationship between language and thought is very complicated, and is approached in different ways by different authors. No systematic discussion of the relationship will be attempted in this monograph. Some points of view advocated by respectively Lashley and Merleau-Ponty, however, will be briefly discussed, since these two authors represent rather divergent opinions.

Lashley (1951) seems to accept the view that some idea or thought precedes any internal or overt expressions. Thought is, in a way, prior to language. He maintains, further, that "the set or the idea does not have a temporal order; that all of its elements are contemporal" (p. 117). He thus adopts a position earlier expressed by Pick (ref. by Lashley). If this is so, the simultaneous structure of thought must be transformed into a temporal structure when thoughts are to be communicated. The listener, on the other hand, is exposed to a temporally organized string of words, and his task thus seems to be to map this temporal structure into a simultaneous cognitive structure again.

What are the implications of such a view for an analysis of order effects? When thought is viewed as a-temporal and prior to language, communication of thoughts should be rather similar to communication concerning outer states of affairs. The speaker would be confronted with similar options when word sequence is to be determined. In principle, then, the nature of sequence problems should remain the same whether we try to make known our thoughts or inform others about particular external states of affairs.

The position of Merleau-Ponty is different from that of Lashley. To him, thought is neither *prior to*—nor *independent of*—language. The following quotation illustrates this point (Merleau-Ponty, 1962, p. 177, see also quotation on p. 23).

> If speech presupposed thought, if talking were primarily a matter of meeting the object through a cognitive intention or through a representation, we could not understand why thought tends towards expression as towards its completion, why the most familiar thing appears indeterminate as long as we have not recalled its name, why the thinking subject himself is in a kind of ignorance of his thoughts so long as he has not formulated them

for himself, or even spoken or written them, as is shown by the example of so many writers who begin a book without knowing exactly what they are going to put into it. A thought limited to existing for itself, independently of the constraints of speech and communication, would no sooner appear than it would sink into the unconscious which means that it would not exist even for itself.

For Merleau-Ponty language and thought are interdependent, or, to use one of his own expressions (*ibid.* p. 183): "thought and expression, then, are simultaneously constituted". Thought is not something a-temporal and in some sense already finished. It is created as pertinent expressions are found.[1] One reservation is required, however: The "identity" of language and thought applies only to what he calls authentic speech, that is (*ibid.* p. 178, Footnote): "speech, which formulates for the first time". Merleau-Ponty thus offers a much more dynamic view of thought than Lashley.

This outlook on the relationship between language and thought also seems to have significant implications for problems of order. The problem is no longer how one fixed, simultaneously or a-temporal structure should be transformed into a temporal structure, but rather which words and sequences can *fulfil or develop the intention of the speaker*. This intention is described as "a void of consciousness", "a momentary desire" or "a certain lack which is asking to be made good", by Merleau-Ponty (*ibid.* p. 183).

But although Merleau-Ponty and Lashley advocate divergent opinions regarding the relationship between language and thought, the expressions used by Merleau-Ponty in the above quotations seem intuitively rather similar to those used by Lashley to describe the thought which precedes language. Thus Lashley, adopting the point of view of the Würzburg School (see, for example, Boring, 1957), maintains (1951, p. 117):

> Thought is neither muscular contraction, nor image, but can only be inferred as a "determining tendency". At most, it is discovered as a vague feeling of pregnancy, of being about to have an idea.

The "vague feeling of pregnancy" appears to be fixed and finished, however, while "the lack which is asking to be made good" has still not attained its form. It is this difference that accounts for the difference in order problems.

1. For some observations which seem to be in conflict with such a view, see Rommetveit (1972 a, footnote p. 232).

One particular consequence of Merleau-Ponty's outlook is that option of order may be examined in terms of consequences on the part of the *speaker* as well as the *listener*. Consider, for instance, two utterances representing alternative sequences of the same set of words. If in such a case one specific sequence of words is chosen, then the *thought constituted* as well as *what is understood by the listener* should be different from what would be the case if exactly the same words were used in the other sequence.

Inherent in this reasoning, however, is the presupposition that Merleau-Ponty recognize sequence as an important factor, and this is clearly revealed in the following quotation using the model of an automatic telephone to illustrate a much more general phenomenon (1965, p. 114):

> Here, as in the organism, it can be said that the excitant—that which puts the apparatus in operation and determines the nature of its responses—is not a sum of partial stimuli, because a sum is indifferent to the order of its factors, rather it is a constellation, an order, a whole, which gives its momentary meaning to each of the local excitations.

The dynamic character of Merleau-Ponty's expositions is appreciated by this author. An integration of his approach and the conceptual framework adopted in the present work seems problematic, however. On the one hand, the basic complementarity between speaker and listener is certainly recognized by Merleau-Ponty. He has, on the other hand, hardly provided us with concepts which take care of the *commonality* between speaker and listener which appears to be a prerequisite for successful anticipatory decoding and listening on the premises of the speaker. Merleau-Ponty's position may hence be said to be subjectivistic, with too much emphasis on the private worlds of each participant (Rommetveit, 1974).

Sequence problems are encountered in modified versions as soon as attention is shifted from *oral* to *written* language. The latter shift implies a change from a *rapidly fading medium* to a medium characterized by relative *permanence*. Oral language is a medium in which the sequence of production is identical to that of information intake on the part of the listener, whereas it in written language is necessary to differentiate between *sequence of production* and *sequence of final result*.

This last point is in need of some further clarification. When written language is considered, it is not necessary for the reader to be acquainted with the processes leading up to the final result. These may remain private affairs, and it should in principle be without importance for the reader in which sequence the different parts or elements had been finished as long as the result remains the same. As a listener to oral language, however, he must attend to the production *as it proceeds*. If something has to be corrected by the speaker for example, the listener will know every try. It is like looking at the author at work, and not only at his final result.

This differentiation between sequence of production and sequence of final result splits the problems of order in written language in two. First, it is possible to ask *what factors influence the sequence of production*, and what *consequences the choice of one particular sequence may have*. The consequences we have been concerned with so far pertain primarily to the author himself in that what exists at a specific point in production may probably affect what he tries to express. Second, and more important in this connection: It is also possible to ask *what factors influence the sequences inherent in the final result and how different sequences affect the reader*.

It is only when we turn to the second set of problems that the concepts of anticipatory decoding and understanding on the premises of the author become of immediate relevance. The author may order information in particular ways because he expects that just such a specific order will have the effects that he wants to establish. One point is important in this connection, however. Just as the writer in a way becomes more independent than the speaker because aspects of his production may remain private, the reader also becomes a more autonomous agent than the listener.

The speaker's *control* over the sequence of information intake by the listener implies to some extent also control of decoding processes. But the same sort of strict control cannot be exerted by the writer. His readers may very well take in information in idiosyncratic ways. They may for example employ scanning procedures in order to find words providing them with important information, instead of adhering to a sequence of information intake involving retroaction and heavy strains upon memory. The permanence of the material also makes it possible to renew information intake and correct misunderstandings by returning to previous parts of the written material. Thus, although a specific sequence may be rather well planned and influenced by anticipatory decoding, the writer never knows to what extent his intentions will be fulfilled because he has not enough control of sequence of information intake.

In writing, the r. reorders time

In the above discussion, we have primarily had shorter segments of written material such as the description of our secretary in mind. Attention may also be directed towards longer segments of material, however, for example towards a whole novel and the sequence in which its different topics are introduced. The impact of the writer becomes in such cases probably more prominent in that the sequence of information intake on that level most often follows the macro-sequence he has provided. (For a discussion of some of the consequences connected to different sequences, see Rommetveit, 1974.) If the reader wishes, however, he may certainly also break such sequencing. Many a reader has turned towards the last pages of a detective or crime story when the intrigue has become too thrilling. He then no longer reads on the premises of the author.

To paint *a picture* may in many cases be conceived of as an act of communication. As such, complementarity between painter and spectator should be of importance. The communication aspect, as well as the permanent character of the product make it reasonable to expect that sequence problems involved may have something in common with those encountered in relation to written language. Because of the permanence, the sequence problems must again be split in two, one set concerning sequence of production, the other set concerning "sequence of final result".

The first set of questions is dealt with in the following quotation from Merleau-Ponty (1962, p. 183):

> Aesthetic expression confers on what it expresses an existence in itself, installs it in nature as a thing perceived and accessible to all, or conversely plucks the signs themselves—the person of the actor, or the colours and canvas of the painter—from their empirical existence and bears them off into another world. No one will deny that here the process of expression brings the meaning into being or makes it effective, and does not merely translate it. It is no different, despite what may appear to be the case, with the expression of thoughts in speech.

The process of production thus becomes in itself very important in cases of pictures as well as in cases of language when examined from the general position of Merleau-Ponty.

As we turn to the second set of questions, *complementarity* between the painter and his spectators should become more crucial, as is also the case in written language. "Sequence of final result" was deliberately put in quotation marks when these problems were introduced, because the final result of the painter, the picture, is first of all characterized by a *spatial structure*. It is the effect of this structure on the spectator that the painter may want to anticipate. Important aspects of this effect, however, may be mediated by sequence of information intake. The point is that the painter by a particular spatial composition may influence—and wish to influence—the movements of the spectator's eyes across the canvas.

It could be expected that the painter had still less control over sequence of information intake than the author. This raises complicated questions, however, because the reader does not normally proceed in a regular fashion from left to right, from top to bottom of a page, as we probably expect. Photographs of eye fixations of readers display, on the contrary, many irregularities, and may in some cases show that readers even break the "rule" of reading first one page, then the next (Kolers, 1973).

We have in our discussion of sequence problems tried to relate the specific sequence problems we shall deal with in the experimental part of this work to presumably similar problems encountered within other fields. Although the approach has been highly elective in the attention has been directed almost exclusively towards visual perception and written language in addition to oral language, the material is sufficient for some reflections.

A whole set of sequence problems has been encountered:

(a) What determines sequence of production?
(b) What sort of consequences does sequence of production have for the producer himself?
(c) What determines temporal or spatial structure of final result?
(d) What determines sequence of information intake?
(e) What sort of consequences is connected to different sequences of information intake?

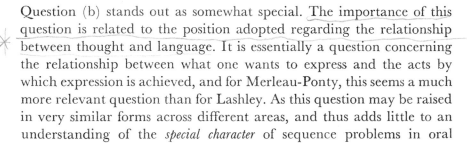

Question (b) stands out as somewhat special. The importance of this question is related to the position adopted regarding the relationship between thought and language. It is essentially a question concerning the relationship between what one wants to express and the acts by which expression is achieved, and for Merleau-Ponty, this seems a much more relevant question than for Lashley. As this question may be raised in very similar forms across different areas, and thus adds little to an understanding of the *special character* of sequence problems in oral language, however, it will not be given further consideration in this book.

The remaining problems seem to appear in somewhat different forms within different areas. In the area of central interest in this monograph, oral language, the relationships between questions may be summarized in the following way: Optional sequence of production is most probably related to the consequences of different sequences through anticipatory decoding. Sequence of production is, moreover, identical to sequence of the final result, which again is identical to sequence of information intake. The specific interrelationship between sequence problems in oral language thus depends on the two factors we have repeatedly emphasized:

1. Oral language is used in *communication situations* in which the producer intends to convey something to the receiver.
2. Oral language is a rapidly fading medium giving the sender control over sequence of information intake.

As soon as these conditions change, the relationship between problems of sequence will also change. Effects of change in condition 2 have already been exemplified by reference to sequence problems in painting and written language. Effects of change in condition 1 can be illustrated by the following example: If the communication aspect disappears as when I no longer listen to my husband talking, but only listen to the sounds he necessarily has to make when working with pottery, his sequence of soundmaking activities will no longer be influenced by anticipatory decoding. In such a case, different factors would be important if we want to understand why one specific sequence of soundmaking activities is initiated. This is the case even though the specific sequence of sounds heard certainly may provide considerable information about what is going on.

Moreover, the activities most similar to oral language as far as sequence problems are concerned, should also be characterized by *being acts of communication* and by *the producer's control of sequence of information intake*. One activity fullfilling these requirements is music.

Our aim in this part has been to view the nature of the more restricted set of sequence problems to be explored within a somewhat broader frame, and so far we have only outlined a skeleton of problems without trying to fill in what might be known already in terms of partial answers. For oral language, however, it is important to search more systematically for answers or possible approaches of relevance when language is considered with due attention of the time dimension. To such a search we now turn.

2.3. In search of the dimension of time in recent studies of language

Recent approaches to language may be characterized by a tendency to detemporalize events (Rommetveit, 1974, p. 9). Few arguments have been given in support of this conclusion, however, and we shall now try to defend it.

Two important aspects of language which become highlighted when due attention is paid to its time dimension, can be exemplified by a quotation from Lotman (1971, p. 38):

> Every experience of a meaning constitutes a separate syncronic field, yet within it are contained the memory of antecedent and consciousness of possible future senses. (Translation: Rommetveit, 1974)

First, what is said *now* is influenced by what was said *earlier*, and will also possibly be modified or enriched by what is *still to come*. If this is so—which seems very reasonable from common sense experience—*it presupposes a conception of word which leaves the word open for contextual modification.* If word meanings are conceived of as rather fixed or invariable, with a one-to-one correspondance between word form and meaning processing, attention towards antecedent and future events becomes of less importance. *There seems thus to be a definite relationship between conceptions of word meaning and extent to which the dimension of time is made a legitimate and significant focus of inquiry.*

A second aspect highlighted by the quotation from Lotman is that what is understood at present is dependent on *memory* of antecedent events. By emphasizing the time dimension in language processing we are compelled to reflect upon the relationship between such processing and memory, since memory seems to be one of the concepts in general psychology with the most obligatory and direct reference to time.[1]

The search for the time dimension will therefore proceed in two main directions. First, an attempt will be made to disentangle the conceptions of word meanings inherent in recent linguistic and psycholinguistic approaches in order to explore what possibilities are left open within the theoretical frameworks for the influence of context. Thereafter,

1. Cf, however, Kvale's (1974 c) discussion of "The temporality of memory".

attention will be directed towards the ways in which memory is dealt with within such frameworks. Fillenbaum's (1971) review of psycholinguistics contains one part called "Processing in real time", and the latter is almost exclusively concerned with problems of hesitation, pauses and breathing as exemplified in the studies by Goldman-Eisler (1968). The problems discussed in relation to the time dimension by Fillenbaum is thus rather different from the problems to be discussed here.

2.3.1. CONCEPTION OF WORD MEANING IN RECENT LINGUISTIC AND PSYCHOLINGUISTIC STUDIES

The linguistic theory that has influenced recent psychology most strongly is the transformational-generative-grammar of Chomsky. The collaboration between the psychologist George A. Miller and Chomsky has been very important in this development (Fillenbaum, 1971, 1973). The collaboration between these scholars and other linguists, psychologists and philosophers of language at Harvard and Massachusetts Institute of Technology (M.I.T.), marked the beginning of a more active interest of psychologists in linguistics and of linguists in psychology. A new term, "psycholinguistics" became the label of the area of common interest.

Chomsky himself has revised his theoretical formulations several times since his first highly influential "Syntactic Structures" appeared in 1957, and somewhat divergent opinions are also currently advocated by linguists and psycholinguists strongly influenced by Chomsky's general framework. The over-all impact of transformational grammar has been so formidable, however, that Rommetveit, for example, talks about the Harvard–M.I.T. school of linguistics and psycholinguistics (see for example Rommetveit, 1974).

In the following discussion of conceptions of word meaning we shall mainly consider the Harvard–M.I.T. school and its ramifications. As Chomsky's own formulations have changed, moreover, our search for conceptions of word meanings will focus primarily on more recent formulations. The discussion relies rather heavily on works by Rommetveit (1972a, b, c, 1974). Some knowledge of Chomsky's position will be presupposed in the discussion. The uninformed reader may be referred to Lyons (1970).

In his critical discussion of the Harvard–M.I.T. school, Rommetveit has also searched for explicit or implicit commitments to a specific

philosophy of language (see especially 1972a, 1974). His conclusion is
that the proponents of the school seem to commit themselves to what
might be called a "picture theory" of language (Rommetveit, 1974,
p. 7):

> Subtle theoretical commitments seem to be involved, however, as soon as
> reference is made to "readings" of sentences and to *synonymy salva veritate*.
> These commitments have to do with what I previously have labelled a
> tacit "picture theory" of language use (Rommetveit, 1972, a, b), and they
> are becoming more and more visible as scholars of the Harvard-M.I.T.
> school expand their operations from *syntax* via *semantics* into linguistic and
> extra-linguistic *presuppositions*, i.e. from explication of syntactic form to
> actual language use.

What then characterizes a "picture theory" of language? We shall not
attempt to give a detailed and philosophically sophisticated answer to
this question, but rather try to outline the main assumptions involved in
a "picture approach". Language is assumed to depict outer states of
affairs, and one essential perspective on language is to decide if utterances depict "reality" in a true or false way. In order to test true/false-
values, utterances are decomposed into propositions. The main
characteristic of propositions is that it should—in principle at least—be
possible to test them against outer states of affairs. The propositions are
true if they are in correspondance with "facts", false if they do not
correspond. The conclusion, true *or* false, should also remain the same
across different contexts. This is a prerequisite for assigning unequivocal
truth values to composite expressions in which single "atomic propositions" are concatenated by logical operators. Wittgenstein's first theory
of language, formulated in Tractatus Logico-philosophicus from 1922,
can thus be called a "picture theory" (Malcolm, 1967).

To clarify the notion of proposition as applied in analysis of ordinary
language somewhat further, we shall resort to an example used by
Rommetveit, showing how an utterance may be decomposed into propositions. The utterance THE OLD MAN IS POOR may be decomposed into the propositions

(a) THE MAN IS OLD, and
(b) THE MAN IS POOR

For both (a) and (b) it should then be possible to test them against
outer states of affairs and decide if they are true or false. To be able to
judge the propositions as *either* true or false, however, would require

xed rules relating one particular word to a specific class or category of outer events. It would, for example, be necessary to decide how many years a thing has to be in order to be called OLD. Without such fixed rules, we would not be able to assign unequivocal truth values to propositions.

We notice already at this point that such a requirement of fixed rules does not correspond to ordinary language use. It seems meaningless to define OLD in terms of specific number of years. When used to characterize a fossile, OLD implies a number of years incomparable to that implied when OLD is used to characterize a man. Or, to use a less extreme example, it seems reasonable to call a man of 60 years OLD when he is in company with people around 30, whereas he would hardly be called OLD if he were visiting a hospital ward with geriatric patients. According to ordinary language usage, then, the statement THE MAN IS OLD would be characterized as "true" in the first case, "false" in the other, although the very same man is described in both cases.

We have maintained that unequivocal judgement of truth values requires fixed rules relating words to categories of outer states of affairs. These outer categories, then, become "real" in a way, they represent *"the one way"* in which the world should be categorized whenever we talk about it. Thus, assumptions about "conceptual realities" are closely related to requirements of fixed rules. This connection is emphasized in a passage by Rommetveit where he maintains that assumptions about "conceptual realities" are necessary for unequivocal criteria for determining truth values (1974, p. 19):

> Such criteria can only be established by adventurous assumptions concerning a *finite and already known universe of "conceptual realities"* of some sort, against which the "real" or "underlying" meanings of words such as BUY, SELL, THINK, and UNCLE can be validated. Such a universe—whatever its epistemological foundation might be—is then imposed upon acts of speech, and what is said can hence be described as true or false representations of composite nonlinguistic states of affairs.

A "picture theory", then, is characterized by commitments to "conceptual realities" and fixed rules for word meanings. If word meaning is defined in terms of a one-to-one correspondence with outer states of affairs, the possible influence upon word meaning of what precedes and what is still to come, is greatly reduced. The dimension of time becomes accordingly of less importance. Our preliminary conclusion at this point, then, is that some of the main reasons for being attentive towards him are eliminated by the assumptions inherent in a picture theory.

Thus, commitment to a picture theory makes for detemporalization, and let us now review some of the arguments given by Rommetveit for his conclusion regarding the Harvard–M.I.T. scholars tacit commitment to such a theory.

In the fifties and early sixties, Chomsky's approach to language was to study what language *is*, not how language was *used* (Chomsky, 1968, p. 62):

> If we hope to understand human language and the psychological capacities on which it rests, we must first ask what it is, not how or for what purposes it is used.

Rommetveit has repeatedly emphasized that utterances must be examined in communication settings, that is, *in use* (Rommetveit, 1968, 1972a, b, c, 1974). This position makes it reasonable to ask: When Chomsky maintained that he was to study what language *is*, would not such a program necessarily imply *implicit assumptions about use*? And if so, what kind of assumptions about use can be detected in the earlier approach by Chomsky and other scholars within the Harvard–M.I.T. group?

Clues to an answer can possibly be found if sentences judged as "ungrammatical" or "anomalous" by this group are examined. Rommetveit, after having performed such an examination, concludes that sentences are judged as "anomalous" if they do not correspond to propositional use (Rommetveit, 1974, p. 14):

> A careful examination of these and a great variety of other rejected cases leaves us with little doubt: The domain of usage presupposed in the Harvard-M.I.T. school's judgement of "grammaticalness" or "sense" is simply propositional use, and judgements have been passed on propositional properties of sentences on the assumption that such properties can be assessed for sentences *in vacuo*. Thus, "My spinster aunt is an infant" is anomalous in the sense that—assuming invariant and mutually irreconsilable truth values for "spinster" and "infant"—it can be interpreted as a composite and contradictory propositional expression. And "I bought sincerity a grief ago" deviates from propositional norms in several ways: it will clearly be impossible to assess unequivocal truth values for sentences containing the word "grief" if the latter is allowed to depict "underlying conceptual realities" of either mood or temporal duration or both. Similar problems arise in connection with "bought sincerity".

look carefully

Thus, to scrutinize one of the examples once more, it is only possible to judge MY SPINSTER AUNT IS AN INFANT (which is an example taken from Katz and Fodor, 1963) as anomalous and contradictory as such, out of context, if it is assumed that SPINSTER always refers to a fixed and finite class of grown-up women and INFANT conversely always refers to a fixed class of children. That is, fixed rules for relating word forms to meaning processes (and, more particularly: to acts of reference) are clearly presupposed in this case, as well as in the other cases discussed by Rommetveit.

It might at first seem unjustifiable to claim that the semantic theory of Katz and Fodor (*ibid.*) could be characterized by fixed rules relating word form to meaning processes, however. An important notion in their theory is that of "selection restriction". Semantic relations between morphemes in a sentence might restrict the number of interpretations possible for a particular word. Thus, PAID in the sentence THE BILL IS LARGE BUT NEED NOT BE PAID restricts the number of interpretations possible for BILL in isolation. The notion of "selection restriction" conceptualize only some rather special aspects of contextual influence among words, however, and cannot account for contextual influences in general. Such an account would also fall outside the scope of semantic theory, according to Katz and Fodor. In spite of "selection restriction", then, fixed rules relating word forms to meaning processes seem to be an outstanding characteristic of their theory.

Additional support for the conclusion about commitment to a picture theory can be found in the different ways in which "deep structure" is explicated. Rommetveit has argued that the descriptions of "deep structures" are characterized by ad hoc procedures, and that different kinds of principles are applied (see especially 1972a). Some of the principles are borrowed from analysis of surface structure, other principles are those of categorial grammar, and still others indicate that "deep structure" is conceived of as intimately related to the propositional content of the sentence. Both of the last two sets of principles contain elements of a picture theory in that they contain assumptions concerning "forms" or "underlying structures" within the sentence that can be said to be isomorphic with event structures.

Let us now examine how "deep structure" is related to the propositional content. As earlier noticed (p. 28) complex propositions may be dissolved into simple propositions to which unequivocal truth values may be assigned. Similarly, complex sentences are dissolved into simple constituent sentences which in principle might be tested against outer states of affairs. Thus, given the sentence THE OLD MAN IS POOR, its "deep structure" may be said to contain the two sentences THE MAN IS OLD and THE MAN IS POOR. Let us now disregard the difficulties concerning unequivocal truth values for, e.g. OLD and POOR and consider other problems having to do with such a dissolution of one composite into two simple sentences.

The dissolution makes it seems as if the two components, THE MAN IS OLD and THE MAN IS POOR, function in the same way within the initial composite sentence: It is asserted that *the man is old* and that *he is poor*. If a truth value should be requested for the composite sentence, the two components should hence be juxtaposed and of equal relevance. Such an analysis fails to capture significant aspects of ordinary language use, however. This is clearly seen once the initial sentence is examined in an ordinary, though imagined communication situation.

Two friends are just about to leave a football-match. On their way out they pass a group of people, and one of them, an old man, is seen picking up empty bottles that have been left among the benches. THE OLD MAN IS POOR is then uttered by one of the friends to the other.

What is asserted in this case seems to be that one particular man is poor. It is certainly reasonable to ask if this is true or not. The man might actually be a miser, with a lot of money put away in a chest. The first part of the sentence, THE OLD MAN, however, does not seem to contain any assertion at all. Its function is to make the participants in the communication act focus upon the same man. What is important in this connection is not whether the man is old in any "real" sense or not, but whether this very expression suffices to establish convergence onto *the same man*.

Differential functions of different parts within the sentence are types of problems that Chomsky and other proponents of the Harvard–M.I.T. school try to incorporate in their most recent formulations, in which problems of language *use* also are seriously considered. This recent development can also be characterized as a development from the study of the sentence in vacuo toward an examination of the sentence in a context. Chomsky has, in his presentation of his new position, used the concepts "focus" and "presupposition", and only part of the sentence, the "focus" is now conceived of as being asserted (1972, p. 100).

Each sentence, then, is associated with a class of pairs (F, P) where F is a focus and P a presupposition, each such pair corresponding to one possible interpretation.

A point of main interest to us in the present context is whether this change in approach also implies a radically revised outlook on semantics and word meaning. According to Rommetveit (1974, p. 15) this is not the case:

> What remains unchanged and shared across all recently developed expansions and ramifications of the Harvard-M.I.T. approach, however, is a primary concern with propositional forms and content of what is said.

Rommetveit supports his conclusion by a close examination of examples used by Fillmore, Lakoff and Chomsky. In what follows, we want to support the conclusion by analysing another example from Fillmore (1972):

He talks about converse relationships between different pairs of words like, for example, LIKE/PLEASE, SELL/BUY, ROB/STEAL. That these pairs are converse implies that sentence pairs as

JOHN LIKES ROSES and
ROSES PLEASE JOHN,

JOHN SELLS ROSES TO SCHOOLGIRLS and
SCHOOLGIRLS BUY ROSES FROM JOHN,

HARVEY ROBS JOHN OF ROSES and
HARVEY STEALS ROSES FROM JOHN

are claimed to be synonymous salva veritate.

Another example of a converse pair offered by Fillmore (1972, p. 8) is TEACH/LEARN. We may hence make up another pair of sentences that, according to the examples given above, also should be synonymous:

JOHN TEACHES HISTORY TO CHILDREN
CHILDREN LEARN HISTORY FROM JOHN

It is not difficult to find situations, however, where one of these expressions would be true, but not the other. If somebody asked John's wife what was John's work at present, she might very well answer: JOHN TEACHES HISTORY TO CHILDREN. It cannot be implied in this case that any single child has ever learned any history from John. John might be an extremely poor teacher that never managed to teach anybody anything. Or the case might be that he just had his first lesson which he would use only to get to know the children. Absolute judgements of converse relationships between words are only possible if fixed word meanings are assumed. When word meaning is considered only partially determined, such absolute judgements become impossible.

After this review of arguments for the conclusion that the proponents of the Harvard–M.I.T. school commit themselves to a "picture theory" of language, the author feels confident to join Rommetveit in his conclusion. The use of language presupposed in their approach is propositional usage, with an implicit conception of word meaning as fixed or invariant rather than only partially determined and open to contextual modification. The rationalism of Chomsky (1968) inherent in his search for universals in language testifies, moreover, to adherence to "conceptual realities".

In his review of psycholinguistics, Fillenbaum (1971) comments on basic assumptions about the meaning of sentences and words in recent work in linguistics and psycholinguistics. His conclusion seems to agree with what has been claimed above, since a common denominator of the works he has surveyed appeared to be a conception of word meaning as invariant entities. To quote (p. 290):

> A basic assumption of recent work is that "the meaning of a sentence is derived from the meanings of its constituent phrases which in turn are derived from the meanings of the words which compose them" *and that the meaning of each of the words involved is a compositional function of some more primitive semantic features or components.*

(Italics mine)

Word meanings are thus explicated as constellations of more primitive semantic features, and nothing is said about contextual modification.

To summarize some main points of the previous discussion: A picture theory of language is characterized by commitment to a conception of word meaning as fixed or invariable. Such a conception is a prerequisite if unequivocal truth values should be assigned to propositions. By adherence to such a conception, the possible influence upon word meanings of what preceeds and what is still to come is greatly reduced. The dimension of time becomes thus of less importance and a picture theory makes in this sense for detemporalization.

A tacit commitment to such a theory by Harvard–M.I.T. scholars is revealed by an examination of implicit assumptions about use presupposed when sentences are judged as "ungrammatical", "anomalous" or "synonymous salva veritate". The domain of usage presupposed is propositional use.

In 1967, Uhlenbeck maintained that transformational theory had failed to grasp "the dynamics of word meaning and its fundamentally 'open' character." (1967, p. 302.) In 1976 it seems still reasonable to join Uhlenbeck in this statement.

2.3.2. LANGUAGE PROCESSING AND MEMORY

Language processing takes place in real time. The first and last part of a phrase, a sentence or a book are separated in time. As first and last parts interact and are parts of one whole, it is necessary that information about earlier parts is retained in order to influence, and also be influenced by, what is to come later. The significance of memory in language processing deserves therefore close attention. The present aim is to explore how memory problems are approached in recent studies of language.

Of particular relevance in this connection is Chomsky's distinction between *competence* and *performance* (Chomsky, 1965). Linguistic theory is in his opinion first of all directed towards an explication of competence, and the latter can be described as the ideal speaker-hearer's intuitive knowledge of his language. Performance, on the other hand, refers to actual language use in concrete situations. According to Chomsky, moreover, memory processes are of no relevance for studies of competence. To quote (1965, p. 3):

> Linguistic theory is concerned primarily with an ideal speaker-listener, in a completely homogenous speech-community, who knows its language perfectly and is *unaffected by such grammatically irrelevant conditions as memory limitations, distractions, shifts of attention and interests, and errors* (random or characteristic) in applying his knowledge of the language in actual performance.

(Italics mine)

Scholars engaged in explorations of competence need therefore pay no attention to memory. The explicit disregard of memory is another unequivocal symptom of detemporalization.

The approach to language as competence, as abstract knowledge, is possible only by systematic detemporalizing of events. Great attention is then directed toward syntactic structures, surface structures and deep structures. Such structures are assigned to sentences detached from use and deprived of their time dimension. The structures thus assigned must be conceived of as simultaneous, or a-temporal structures.

While memory is irrelevant as far as competence is concerned, it cannot so easily be defined out of performance. How, then, are memory processes discussed in studies of performance?

Memory tasks have been used in many psycholinguistic experiments. (E.g. Mehler, 1963; Savin and Perchonock, 1965; Johnson, 1965; Blumenthal, 1967; Blumenthal and Boakes, 1967.) Fillenbaum (1973) discusses some selected studies where memorial techniques have been used. Such tech niques have seldom been used because of primary interest in memory processes as such, however, although some of the questions posed suggest a more serious concern about memory (Mehler, 1963; Savin and Perchonock, 1965). The primary interest has nevertheless been geared towards exploration of possible psychological consequences of linguistically defined structures (Fillenbaum, *ibid.*).

Memory thus comes in because performance on memory tasks is supposed to be affected by variations in linguistic structures. More detailed explorations of the relationship between language processing and memory processes are difficult to find. Fillenbaum has pointed out this lack of contact between psycholinguistics and studies of memory (1971, 1973). In his review of psycholinguistics he maintains (1971, p. 254):

> With regard to most attempts at (fragments of) a performance model, one thing is rather striking—there has been very little recourse to what is generally known about attentive mechanisms, short term and longer term memorial processes, temporal constraints on information processing, etc.

This lack of interest in memory processing as such even in performance studies further strengthens the conclusion about the prevailing tendency to detemporalize language in recent psycholinguistic research. It is remarkable that memory tasks, in themselves with such a clear reference to time, in many cases are used exclusively to give information about a-temporal structures.

In the above, attention was directed towards studies influenced mainly by transformational-generative grammar. Some discussions initiated by representatives of other traditions, however, are also of relevance. Glanzer (1972) raises the problem of the relationship between short-term store and language processing rather directly in an article about storage mechanisms in recall. The problems discussed are the greater efficiency in storing of auditory as compared to visual material in short-term store, the effect of grouping and the question of what sort of units are held in short-term store. It should also be noted that Glanzer in this article refers to Yngve (1960) as the one who first explored the relationship between language processing and short-term store in a constructive manner. It is also of interest that short term tasks are included in test batteries used for the testing of language abilities. The Illinois Test of Psycholinguistic Abilities (Kirk, McCarthy and Kirk, 1968) includes one test for auditory and one test for visual short-term memory.

In this connection, the attempt by Goodglass, Gleason and Hyde (1970) to explore different dimensions of auditory language comprehension in aphasia is also of relevance. Among the different tasks used in this study was also one called Pointing-Span Test. This test was similar to tests of memory span. But to avoid talking, the response of the subjects was to point to appropriate pictures. One of the aims of this study was to compare the performance of different diagnostic groups within aphasia. Five different diagnostic groups were used, Broca's, Wernicke's, conduction, anomic and global aphasia. For a discussion of the characteristics of each group, see Goodglass and Kaplan (1972).

Only one of the results from this study will be discussed here. It was found that the patients with Bocha's aphasia had the lowest score on the Pointing-Span Test with a mean of 2·36. At the same time this special group is clinically characterized by good comprehension. It seems then to be possible to understand, in the words of Goodglass et al. (1970, p. 605), "rather long and quite involved sentences" and at the same time have an extremely low memory-span. This result seems rather surprising to this author and seems also to be in contrast with a remark on language and short-term memory given by Waugh and Norman (1965):

> Indeed we believe that it would be impossible to understand or to generate a grammatical utterance if we lacked this rather remarkable mnemonic capacity.

Results such as those presented by Goodglass et al. provide additional support to the claim that the relationship between language processing and memory ought to be given attention. The relationships might very well turn out to be different from what was expected. The present increasing interest in this problem area is encouraging (Herriot, 1974; Kintsch, 1974).

3

The Open and Dynamic Character of Words

In the preceding discussion it was maintained that there seems to be a relationship between conception of word meaning and concern with the dimension of time. When word meanings are assumed to be invariable, it is reasonable to focus less attention on the time dimension—on what precedes and what is still to come—than when word meanings are conceived of as open; that is, susceptible to contextual modification. *A conception of word meaning as open is thus part of our rationale for a close attention to temporality.*

Illustrations of word openness have already been offered, and it has also been claimed that word openness characterizes ordinary language use. What is implied by openness, moreover, has only been superficially discussed. As this issue is of central concern in the present monograph, it has to be further explored. In what follows we want to approach the problem in a somewhat more systematic manner than was possible in Chapter 2.

The heading of this paragraph includes the word "dynamic" in addition to the word "open". The former word refers to the change and modification of meaning over time and is thus used more strongly to emphasize word meaning as always only *partially determined* and therefore susceptible to further modification or enrichment as more information is presented.

The influence upon word meaning of context have been explicitly recognized by different authors. Reference can, for example, be made to Osgood, Suci and Tannenbaum and to G. A. Miller. The former authors maintain (1957, p. 275):

The meaning of a word in ordinary speech is influenced by the context of other words with which it occurs.

The latter maintains (1965, p. 16):

> In isolation most words can have many different meanings; which meaning they take in a particular sentence will depend on the context in which they occur. That is to say, their meaning will depend both on the other words and on their grammatical role in the sentence.

Word conceptions underlying recent studies of language are frequently characterized by analysis of word meaning into more basic semantic features or components (see, for example, Katz and Fodor, 1963). To do justice to previous psycholinguistic work, however, reference should also be made to Osgood's and Noble's approaches to word meaning presented more than twenty years ago. Osgood has primarily been working at what might be called emotive meaning (Osgood, 1952; Osgood, Suci and Tannenbaum, 1957), while Noble's (1952) attention primarily has been directed towards associative meaning. The frame of reference to be used in the following discussion about word meaning is mainly that outlined by Rommetveit (1968, 1972c). His approach to word meaning will be outlined below.

3.1. Rommetveit's approach to problems of word meaning

In linguistic literature, words are often divided into two classes, the *designators* or *content words* and the *formators* or *function words* (Weinreich, 1963). Content words or designators are words with at least some autonomy, or some independent meaning, such as BOY, KINGDOM, DEMOCRACY, RUN, BLUE, GOOD. The function words or formators, on the other hand, must be embedded in some context in order to activate meaning processes. EITHER, OR, BUT, IF are examples of this class.

In psychological studies of word meaning, most attention has been directed toward the content words. The conception of word meaning outlined by Rommetveit (1968, 1972c) is also primarily aimed at an understanding of the content word. His attempt to disentangle components of word meaning is based upon a general description of the meaning processes activated by such a word when presented in isolation.

The view of Rommetveit is presented in condensed form in the following passage (1968, p. 111):

What we propose is a three-component model for processing of words in isolation. An act of reference is postulated as the initial process, followed by a sustained process of representation affecting and affected by an associative and an affective concurrent activity, respectively.

What is believed to happen when an individual is exposed to an isolated word (in spoken or written form) in such a way that meaning processes may develop freely, is roughly as follows: First of all, there must be an act of reference. This means that the word must provide for an orientation toward a special class or category of objects or phenomena. The importance of this orientation becomes more clear when viewed against problems of homonymy. Suppose that the Norwegian word STRENG is presented. This means: (1) Severe—as in A SEVERE FATHER, or (2) String—as in A STRING OF THE GUITAR. If STRENG is to activate meaning processes, the act of reference must be related either to the entity indicated by the English word SEVERE or to objects called STRING in English. Once such an act of reference has been performed affective and associative processes may be activated as well.

In addition to the affective and associative components, a third component is also assumed, the representational one, which may be considered a temporal extension of the act of reference. Rommetveit uses "to represent" as complementary to "to refer". While "to refer" is used as indicating the "reaching out" toward the objects, "to represent" is used to indicate that the objects are "taken in"—or, better—for the processes which in some way make the objects "psychological present".

If it is possible for a subject to ponder the meaning of one word for a certain period of time, a sustained representational process must be assumed. The associative processes, for example, must in one way or another be anchored in representational processes activated by the word via the act of reference. If this were not the case, associative chaining would result, and meaning processes uniquely attached to the specific stimulus word would no longer be secured. Associative chaining means that, e.g. the second response in a sequence of associations would be triggered by the first associative response rather than by the stimulus word. Patterns like   **HORSE** → COW → BULL   would then be observed instead of   **HORSE** → RIDING — COW

The act of reference has priority over other meaning components, both *logically* and from the perspective of *time*. The other meaning components are dependent on the act of reference. It is clear that different associative and affective processes would be activated in the case of STRENG meaning severe and in the case of STRENG meaning string. (See Rommetveit and Strømnes, 1965.) The sustained representational process would also be very different in these cases.

The relationship between components, however, cannot be fully described by this dependence of the representational, the associative, and the emotive component upon the initial act of reference. The sustained representational component is influenced by the associative and the emotive components, and it in turn influences these components. Thus, the three components must be conceived of as activated in close interaction.

To gain information about the different components, the following methods could probably be used: Questions for definitions as well as studies of depth of intention, should give information about the representational component. The associative component might be studied by word-association tasks, and the affective component by the semantic differential (Osgood, Suci, Tannenbaum, 1957). As soon as this is said, however, some reservations must be mentioned. Word association responses may represent very different relations to the stimulus word. Contrast relations, relations of part/whole, and contiguity relations would all be found—just to give some examples. It is not at all certain that all these different kinds of associations yield information of the associative component. Contrast associations, for example, are so closely related to the stimulus word—both serving to encode the same dimension—that they perhaps must be considered as reflections of the intial act of reference rather than of the associative component as tentatively defined above. The difficulty of relating one specific method to one component is also present in connection with the semantic differential (see discussion on pp. 45–46). For more details of such methodological problems, see Rommetveit (1968).

One warning must be given against the dissection of word meaning into different sub-processes: Such a description is not to be taken as a description of an individual's *experience* when a word is presented. Word meaning is certainly experienced much more as a whole; if attended to at all in a reflective, analytic way. The dissection of word meaning into different components, however, serves primarily as a frame of reference for organizing different language phenomena in such a way as to account for the flexibility of word meaning across different contexts.

3.2. Word meaning potentialities

The outline of word meaning given by Rommetveit has been presented as a frame of reference for a discussion about the open and dynamic character of word meaning. In what ways are such a description compatible with the claims of word meaning as open and dynamic? How is the conception of Rommetveit to be understood?

Rommetveit's conception concerns processing of words in isolation, given sufficient time for meaning processes to develop freely. He has provided a formal description, and its concrete realization is supposed to vary. When one word is presented to an individual in an artificial situation like the one described, the direction of processing will be influenced by his recent experiences, his present thoughts and so on, and the processing of different individuals will vary, partly because the meaning processes is affected by different "background" factors.

Our primary aim, however, is to understand processing of words as part of a normal communication situation. In order to make the conception of Rommetveit an instrument toward this end, it is important to understand the differences between the artificial situation of presenting one word to an individual in an experimental situation and an ordinary communication situation. One characteristic feature of the former is that *one word* is presented, while normally *several words* would be received in close temporal succession. The former situation lacks, moreover, *a social dimension*. Processing of words are first of all affected by characteristics of the individual, while the attempt to understand just what the other person intended to convey induce, in addition, a social dimension in the communication situation. In the subsequent discussion, it will be explored how such differences may affect the processing of words.

When a particular word is encountered in a sentence which is used in ordinary conversation, some *reduction* of meaning components activated by the isolated word is to be expected. The word KEY in the following sentence may serve as an example. THE KEY IS BEHIND THE STONE TO THE LEFT OF THE OAK TREE SOUTH OF THE BARN. KEY might in isolation activate representational, associative and affective meaning processes extending over considerable time. If KEY in the message given above were to activate processes of comparable complexity, it would be impossible for the person to pay attention to all additional different details in the message.

The reduction of meaning components is expected, first of all, to affect those parts of the meaning process which occur latest. This means that the sustained representational process as well as the associative and affective processes will be affected. The initial act of reference, however, has to occur. If not, the word would be devoid of information (see, however, further comments on p. 49). Intuitively, this reduction seems reasonable. If your associations lead you to the old and beautiful key in the chest at home when you hear the word KEY in the message above, it will most probably be impossible for you to find the key whose location is being described.

In the description of the processing of the single word, nothing is said about the relative importance of the different meaning components. Language is used as a means to establish intersubjectivity in a great variety of settings, however, and it is reasonable to expect that different components may prevail in different situations. Imagine the following situations where DEMOCRACY has been uttered:

(1) DEMOCRACY WAS INTRODUCED IN NORWAY IN 1814, said in a lecture concerning modern forms of government.

(2) DEMOCRACY—(long pause), BATTLES WERE FOUGHT FOR IDEAS, said by an actor reading a poem.

(3) AS GOOD PARTY MEMBERS WE SHALL ALWAYS REMAIN DEVOTED TO DEMOCRACY, said by the leader of a political party to the party members during a campaign speech.

If intersubjectivity is to be established in these settings, the utterances must, most probably, be interpreted according to somewhat different "rules" (Rommetveit, 1974). What is important in (1), is primarily transmission of novel and factual information. In (2), commonality with respect to associations seems to be of particular importance, while intersubjectivity concerning mood and emotive tone is the primary aim in (3). Thus, the representational component is expected to be the most essential in (1), the associative component in (2), and the affective component in (3).

When a specific word is encountered in some natural context, then, the patterning of meaning processes will as a rule differ from that of, e.g. a laboratory situation in which a single word is presented for some particular purpose. The meaning processes actually activated on any specific occasion will, moreover, be different depending on each particular context. The description of word meaning proposed by Rommetveit cannot be taken to be, and is never intended to be, a description of processes activated in the same way on every occasion. It is to be undestood more as a general frame or as *the most expanded set of possibilities of which only particular subsets most often are activated.* When the description of word meaning offered by Rommetveit is understood in such a way, it is clearly compatible with a conception of word meaning as open.

When this is said, it is tempting to discuss somewhat further what might happen to the different components in different situations. Some of the problems to be discussed are brought to mind by a puzzle which seems inherent in what is said earlier. It was claimed that a reduction of meaning components is to be expected when the word is included in a context. It might be questioned if there is anything left of the representational, the associative, and the emotive components, and thus whether it makes sense to discuss the relative importance of different components in ordinary usage at all.

It is at this stage only possible to offer some speculations concerning these issues. First, it is hardly reasonable to expect that the meaning process usually is constrained to only the minimal act of reference. Most likely, degree of reduction will vary from one type of communication to another. In the example about the key (see p. 42) a person was listening to a message composed almost exclusively of necessary and highly informative and non-redundant words. It was then necessary to be attentive to almost every word in order to be able to find the key later on. In such a case, decoding has to be firmly controlled, and in such a way that the listener must attend equally closely to a number of consecutive words. None of the three examples in which DEMOCRACY was used, however, represents such a message. The distribution of attention during decoding may hence be less constrained, the listener may be more selective in his attention, and in such a way, for instance, that more time and attention may be devoted to those parts of the sentence which are most difficult and/or most essential. In DEMOCRACY WAS INTRODUCED IN NORWAY IN 1914, for example, much attention may be focused on DEMOCRACY. This word is by no means unequivocal with respect to meaning, and at the same time of central significance in the sentence.

In DEMOCRACY—BATTLES WERE FOUGHT FOR IDEAS it

may be the case that the encoder intends to facilitate the decoder's associative activity. Different conditions may be conductive to such facilitation. In (2), it is induced by the long pause following DEMO-CRACY. Consequently, the word is experienced in a condition very close to that of the isolated word. This control of time is only possible in oral language, however.

When the same poem is experienced in a written version, a similar effect may be achieved by spatial arrangements. It is possible, for example, to print only one word on the line or on the page. Another possibility is to incorporate the essential word in a context of words which the author anticipates to be of very little importance. A situation resembling the one described for (1) may then be established. Such means may be used by the author. The receiver, however, also has his means. Because of the permanence of the written material, he may read as slowly as he wishes, giving himself sufficient time for associative activity. Poems represent one particular mode of communication, and without adhering to its "rules" for comprehension, intersubjectivity can hardly be established.

The variable importance of different components within different contexts, may, moreover, pose methodological problems of relevance when the meaning of one particular word is to be explored. This seems to be true for use of the semantic differential. (Osgood, Suci and Tannenbaum, 1957). The semantic differential was described by Osgood in 1952 as a method to measure meaning. This method can shortly be described in the following way: A word (for example LADY, which we may call the stimulus word), as well as different scales are presented to the subjects. These scales all have seven steps, and a pair of polar adjectives defines the endpoints of every such scale. Examples are:

FAIR   —|—|—|—|—|—|— UNFAIR
STRONG   —|—|—|—|—|—|— WEAK
ACTIVE   —|—|—|—|—|—|— PASSIVE

The task is to judge the stimulus word against every scale. The subject's judgements are to be made on the basis of what the stimulus word means to him and are indicated by putting down a checkmark on each scale.

The position of the checkmark is supposed to be dependent upon two factors: (1) which one of the contrast adjectives is most closely related to the stimulus word; and (2) how strong this connection or association is judged to be.

In the following discussion, the stimulus word is to be conceived of as *context*, and it is in the meaning processes activated by the polar adjectives we expect that different components may be central. An example may illustrate this point. If EIFFEL-TOWER and FLY should be judged against the scale BIG/LITTLE it is to be expected that the former would be judged as big, the latter as little. The reason behind this is that the stimulus-words, EIFFEL-TOWER and FLY, primarily seems to activate the representational component of BIG and LITTLE, or, to use the words of Osgood (1962), because the scale BIG/LITTLE is denotatively relevant in this case. If LOVE and SIN should be judged against the same scale, however, these words would most probably activate the affective component triggered by the adjectives. In Osgood's terminology, the scale would then be supposed to be used connotatively.

In practice it is often difficult to decide in which way the scales are used, or, said differently: which component has been the most central. If, for example, DE GAULLE and NAPOLEON were to be judged against the scale BIG/LITTLE, both components might constitute the base for the ratings provided the subjects know the body size of these persons. The check-mark itself will then in many cases convey little information. If DE GAULLE is rated as little and NAPOLEON as big, it must be possible to conclude that the affective component has been in focus. But if DE GAULLE is rated as big, NAPOLEON as little, which component has then been most central in response to the adjectives?

This type of problem is among those referred to (p. 41) in the discussion of possible methods to gain information of different meaning components. Osgood, Suci and Tannenbaum maintain that one should try not to use scales which are denotatively relevant. It is, however, not always easy to identify the nature of the semantic relation between scales and stimulus-words. The relationship may be even more complicated than suggested above (Rommetveit, 1968, p. 159).

The initial act of reference has so far been given little attention. It has only been said to be logically prior to the development of the meaning components and to vary depending on context. The latter point deserves closer attention. In the presentation of Rommetveit's description of word meaning, the lack of one-to-one relationship between word form and act of reference was exemplified by reference to the homonymous word STRENG in Norwegian (p. 40). Homonymous words, however, seem to be of restricted interest in this connection. Nobody claims that these word forms always have the same meaning. But a one-to-one relationship between word form and initial act of reference does not seem to exist for other words either. The act of reference, the "reaching out' towards outer objects or states of affairs appears to be different on different occasions. In other words, one specific word form gives rise to different categorization processes in different contexts.

In the discussion of word conception in recent linguistic and psycholinguistic studies, OLD was given as an example to show how word meaning changed depending on context (p. 29). The number of years implied when a man is called OLD was said to be incomparable to the number of years implied when a fossil is called OLD. This means that the act of reference activated by OLD "reaches out" toward denotatively and quantitatively defined different sets of outer objects in these cases. When the example is as extreme as the one here given, most probably no overlap would be found between the sets. In the case of being old among a group of people of thirty compared to being old at a geriatric ward, the sets will overlap to a great extent. Still, however, some instances will fall within one set, yet outside the other.

When the act of reference is different in different contexts, this may also have another implication. The best way to explain this second possibility may be by way of an example. The word WOMAN (or its plural form WOMEN) can be used. If this word were to be defined, the characteristics human, adult, and female seem to appear essential. It is reasonable to expect that the act of reference triggered by WOMAN in some cases "uses" all of these characteristics in the "reaching out" toward outer objects. In other cases, however, only some of these characteristics become important.

When WOMEN ENTERED THE ROOM is used as the opening passage of a novel, the act of reference triggered by WOMEN would most probably involve all of these characteristics. In a discussion about intellectual differences between men and women, on the other hand, WOMEN in WOMEN ARE OFTEN FOUND TO BE SUPERIOR IN VERBAL ABILITY would trigger a somewhat different act of reference. In this case it may be taken for granted that the discussion is focused upon *grown-up people*, and what is made known by WOMEN is therefore first of all if females or males are superior in this special ability.

That is, WOMEN is used primarily to provide information about sex. Other examples, illustrating situations where the act of reference triggered by WOMEN primarily would involve other defining characteristics, could also be given.

The act of reference triggered by WOMEN differs in the two cases mentioned above. The function of—or *what is made known* by—WOMEN certainly is different. In the case of the novel, every possibility was open until WOMEN was received. When intellectual differences were discussed, it was already known that differences between categories of adult human beings would be the topic.

The acts of reference triggered by WOMEN in the two situations seem, however, to differ in another way from the acts of reference triggered by OLD. The latter difference pertains to the characteristics of the set of outer events to which the words refer. In the case of OLD, it was maintained that these characteristics would be different. In the case of WOMEN, on the other hand, these characteristics could be identical.

When it is said that WOMEN in the discussion about abilities first of all gives information about sex, there is certainly not implied a "reaching out" towards every organism of the female sex. The other characteristics are also present in the sense that they are already taken for granted. When the acts of reference are said to differ, it is because the word WOMEN as such conveys different "portions" of this information in the two cases.

What is said above may be pursued still one step further. Cases may be found where human, female and adult are all known before the word WOMAN is uttered. One example might be an utterance overheard in a discussion about women with professional work: PROFESSOR ANNE HANSEN IS A REAL WOMAN. In such a case, the name and title have already provided the information about the attributes female, human and adult. The sentence, however, seems acceptable, and it does not serve to give redundant information only. What is made known by WOMAN seems to be that Anne Hansen has characteristics very often associated with women, and the contribution of WOMAN must first of all be sought in its potentiality to give information about sex-role aspects.

Partial determination of word meaning may also be illustrated with the example above. If the sentence, for instance, continued: IN RELATION TO CHILDREN, this additional information would further direct, enrich or modify the contribution of WOMAN.

In the previous examples what is made known by WOMAN differs because more or less of its potentialities are already part of what is taken for granted. The information inherent in some words may, however, in other situations appear contradictory to what seems to be conveyed by other words. The following situation illustrates this point. The mother and father of a little girl, five years old, look at her when she puts on her new dress and proudly looks at herself in the mirror, and the father says to the mother: SHE IS ALREADY A LITTLE WOMAN. From the perspective of fixed word meaning it could be said that the adulthood of WOMAN is in conflict with the childhood of SHE in this case. When used in this particular communication setting, however, WOMAN seems to be used because of its possibility to arouse sex-role aspects, and no contradiction is thus involved. The mother's and father's common knowledge of the actual age of the little girl may be said to *overrule* the information of adulthood usually conveyed by WOMAN.

We may safely conclude, therefore, that the act of reference triggered by one specific word changes depending on context. The specific set of outer objects or outer states of affairs to which a particular word refers may vary. The number of "dimensions" or attributes activated may also change from a maximum towards a theoretic minimum, the latter defined by activation of only associative and emotive components.

The possibility to activate only associative and emotive components, however, seems to go contrary to what has been claimed earlier. We have argued that reduced time for processing when a word is included in context may prevent representational, associative and emotive components from developing. The act of reference would always be activated, however, because the words otherwise would be devoid of information (p. 43). Contrary to this, we now claim that only emotive and associative components may be triggered by the word. This would be the case if the information normally provided by the act of reference had already been given, or made irrelevant either by preceding verbal communication or by nonverbal means.

The different examples of how the act of reference change depending on the communication situation, have one common denominator. They illustrate how what is said at each stage is understood *on the basis of what is tacitly taken for granted.* When fossils are the topic, OLD is interpreted in such a way that it expands or modifies what is already known, and the same is true regarding the different meanings that may be conveyed by WOMAN. When one word is presented in isolation, individual characteristics and experiences determine the interpretation of the word. When the same word is part of different communication situations, what is tacitly believed to be common knowledge direct the processing of words. Thus, a definite social dimension is involved in the latter cases. The dependency relation between the interpretation of particular words and what is already taken for granted is further discussed in Message Structure (p. 159).

An abstract totality of all the different meanings and meaning elaborations that could be activated by one specific word, could be called the meaning potentialities of that word. The entire set of word meaning potentialities is never activated in any concrete situation. It can only be approached through a reflective and creative strategy where the superordinate task is to imagine the word included in different contexts. A tentative map of its entire meaning potential may then be elaborated by reflecting upon the different contributions of the word across a variety of contexts. It seems to me that this is the way the notion of "word meaning potentialities" is used by Rommetveit (1968).

An intriguing question may be raised in this connection, however. A word meaning potentiality is certainly a very abstract entity, and in order to explore word openness we may need a more functional concept. It is often necessary to postpone decision, to keep possibilities open. How are words processed in such cases?

It might be suggested that they would only be processed to non-semantic levels. It may on the other hand be argued that only what may be called "inherent decisions" are performed: When OLD is presented, it is immediately known that YOUNG is not meant, and when WOMAN is presented, it is known that MAN is not meant. Such decisions are of a *relational character* as opposed to *positive characterizations* of word meaning (e.g. WOMAN as composed of female, adult and human). Such problems will be pursued further in the discussion of experimental results (p. 138).

3.3. Notes on word autonomy

In the preceding discussion the focus has been on the *open* and *dynamic* character of words. With a heavy emphasis on such characteristics, we may ask whether a specific word form without any context is so vague and open as to mean virtually nothing. It may be argued that words as such do not have a meaning of their own, that they are devoid of autonomy.

When word autonomy is going to be discussed in the present context it will be related to, but not identical to the theme in discussions of the word as a linguistic unit. In linguistic literature it is discussed, for example, if it is reasonable to use the word as a linguistic unit or if the morpheme is all that is needed (Krámský, 1969). Much direct or indirect concern is also given to the problems of *defining* the word, given that it is an acceptable linguistic unit. (Ullmann, 1957; Schultink, 1962; Krámský, 1969). Juilland and Roceric (1972) have written a bibliography of recent work devoted to the study of the linguistic concept of the word. The term "word autonomy" occurs also in linguistic contexts (Ullmann, 1957; Van Wyk, 1968). We shall focus primarily on *semantic aspects of words*, however, whereas both *formal, syntactic and semantic aspects* are considered in linguistic discussions of word autonomy. It is worth noting that the word is accepted as a reasonable concept without further discussion. For arguments for such a decision, see Krámský (1969). The position of Reichling should also be mentioned in this connection. Van Wyk (1968, p. 543) maintains:

> In the second quarter of this century, when modern linguistics was beginning to find its feet, many concepts of traditional grammar were thrown overboard or drastically overhauled. One of the concepts that threatened to become a casualty of this justifiable zeal for renewal was the word. It was then that Prof. Reichling's monumental work, Het Woord (1935), appeared, in which he demonstrated conclusively that the word is an essential linguistic unit without which no language can exist and which is, in fact, the most fundamental of all linguistic units. In a certain sense he saved the word from disappearing from linguistics or being relegated to an inferior position.

To return to the opening question, when words are open and dynamic, can this be taken to imply that words can mean anything?—To the author the answer is clearly no. *Words have autonomy*. The concept of word autonomy is rather complicated, and the subsequent inquiry is not meant to provide any detailed and sufficient account of the problems. It seems very important to the author to explicate her position, however, because the emphasis on concepts like word openness, time dimension, and sequence problems could easily be taken to indicate an extreme view of word openness which is divergent from the position advocated in this monograph.

The most extreme position, that words out of contexts mean nothing, is not accepted. According to Jakobson (1971, p. 79) it has repeatedly been asserted in the theory of language since the early Middle Ages that words out of contexts mean nothing. To Jakobson this seems only to be true for one pathological condition, that is for the specific aphasic disorder which he calls similarity disorder. Bolinger (1963) also discusses the position that meaning is derived from context. He does not accept this view, and notes that such a position is circular because (p. 133) "it defines A in terms of BCD, B in terms of ACD, C in terms of ABD, etc.". The same kind of problem is carefully discussed by Allport (1962) in connection with the question whether a core-context theory could explain meaning in perception.

Unfortunately, however, it is easier to formulate the position which is not acceptable than to present an alternative formulation. Words have autonomy, and words presented alone have meaning. Context influences word meaning, but only within certain limitations. It seems impossible, though, to characterize the limits in any fixed way. Word meaning is open also in the sense that we have to consider communication of genuinely novel experiences.

The position we want to adopt with respect to word autonomy thus seems closely related to that of Reichling. It is difficult to get to know Reichling's view in details, because his writings are mostly in Dutch. In the following quotation from Het Woord (1935, p. 393) both the autonomy and the dependence of the word are emphasized, however:

> Zij (Woord) hebben een eigen wettelikheid, zij hebben een autonomie, zij zijn óók afhankelik; en het is deze verhouding van autonomie en afhankelikheid die om verklaring vraagt.

Reichling's points of view are also revealed through the writing of others. Thus, Uhlenbeck (1967, p. 312) notes how Reichling has stressed both the uniqueness and the dynamic character of word meaning:

> As all students of semantics, Reichling started with the study of appellative words. His theory has stressed what has not yet gained a place in transformational theory: the uniqueness and the dynamic nature of word meaning. Reichling's theory has tried to explain how the meaning of appellative words, understood as a form of knowledge, operates in actual speech; how these words maintain their identity *in spite of the fact that in actual language-use different sub-senses of their meaning may be actualized*, and how

the relation between meaning and thing meant has to be understood. (Italics mine.)

It may perhaps be possible to specify the concept of word autonomy somewhat further. It was claimed that words presented alone have meaning. This expression can be interpreted in at least two different ways. It may refer to presentations of single words as for example in tests of word associations. When the word activates meaning processes in such a situation, however, it may be argued that the word is *not* interpreted out of context. When no context is given, the person is free to create his own.

"Words presented alone" could also refer to a situation where only one word has been presented up to this point, but where a continuation in the communication is to be expected. That is, the "single word" is in this case considered from a communication perspective. This is the way I want to interpret "words presented alone" in this connection. Such an interpretation has implication for the concept of word autonomy. It can be said that a word has some autonomy if some reduction of the universe of meaning potentialities may take place as soon as the one word is presented. When context is given, further restriction takes place. But the point is that the process of restriction or of decision making may start on the basis of the information inherent in one word. It should be noted that the present comments are closely related to the discussion of word meaning potentialities and the question about a more functional concept (p. 50). Perhaps the concepts of word autonomy could serve such a function?

In his discussion of the word as a linguistic unit, Krámský (1969, p. 49) refers to B. Trnka who also seems to hold a view comparable to the one suggested here:

> Thus, according to B. Trnka, if we accept the polysemanticity of words we must ask what gives identity to the word in a language system. For example, shall we see in the form *head* as many different meanings as there are actual utterances or shall we see only one word? The answer, according to Trnka is, *that every word has its basic meaning which in actual utterances is used in different variations of meaning without its basic oppositional meaning fully disappearing.* The variations of meaning connected with the phonological formation head are linked to the basic meaning and not directly to the extralinguistic reality. (Last italics mine.)

A statement that "words have autonomy" must not be taken to mean that autonomy is an all-or-none affair. *Words have more or less autonomy.* No detailed discussion of this problem will be given. The traditional distinction between content words and function words, defining the content words as those with at least some independent meaning (p. 39) suggests immediately, however, that content words would be more autonomous than function words. Such a position has its problems, but they will not be taken up here. To give one concrete example of words differing in autonomy, the two deictic words HE and THIS might be compared. When only HE is given, it is immediately known that someone in singular and of male sex is referred to. When only THIS is given, on the other hand, almost nothing can be known. THIS can be used to refer to almost anything. HE therefore seems to have more autonomy than THIS.

It is tempting, towards the end of these comments on autonomy, to mention a rather different, but relevant, perspective. We have noticed that words are open enough also to be used to communicate new experiences. Such communication of "new experiences" is not without its problems, however, and it may be suggested that part of these problems is connected to the *stability* of word meanings. Blakar (1973) has discussed the problems of communicating about a society with *equality* between the sexes when the words we have to use are trapped in associative networks heavily coloured by existing *differences*. That is, communication seems to be hampered by the fact that words bring with them associations which *should not have been evoked* by the actual context.

Such stability of word meaning, serving a conserving function, thus exemplifies one possible limit to word openness. The stability noticed under such conditions cannot be considered any simple manifestation of word autonomy, however. When we talk about stability, it refers primarily to the relative inflexibility of associative-emotive components, whereas the discussion of word autonomy is primarily directed towards referential aspects. Both aspects, however, carry with them limitations of word openness.

PART II

4

Introduction to the Experiments

4.1. Different decoding strategies

In the experiments to be reported descriptions like the following were used as stimulus material.

I   A SECRETARY WHO IS SEVERE, COOL, EXTRAORDIN-
    ARY, BEAUTIFUL, PLEASANT.
II A SECRETARY WHO IS PLEASANT, BEAUTIFUL, EXTRA-
    ORDINARY, COOL, SEVERE
III A SEVERE, COOL, EXTRAORDINARY, BEAUTIFUL,
    PLEASANT SECRETARY
IV A PLEASANT, BEAUTIFUL, EXTRAORDINARY, COOL,
    SEVERE SECRETARY

These descriptions are different from those discussed earlier in that five adjectives are used, not three.

Forms I and II are similar in that the noun (N) is presented before the qualifying adjectives (A). In forms III and IV, on the other hand, the presentation of the noun is postponed until every adjective has been presented.

It has been suggested that position of noun may influence the decoding process (p. 16). At this point possible decoding strategies for descriptions with noun first and with noun at the end will be discussed, and let us now summarize previous conjectures into some tentative models of decoding strategies.

Forms with noun first (I and II) may be said to allow for a cumulative strategy of processing in which every successive adjective is decoded immediately so as to yield a modified impression of the secretary at each successive stage. This means, for example, that as soon as SEVERE is heard, the latter may immediately be decoded and serve to modify the impression generated by SECRETARY. In the same way, COOL is also immediately decoded and similarly modifies the impression already generated by SECRETARY and SEVERE jointly, and so on.

Forms with noun at the end (II and IV) make for a postponement of decoding of adjectives until the noun has been heard. This is the case because what is made known by each adjective, remains largely undetermined until it is known what sort of entity it describes. Such postponement of decoding implies that the adjectives must be stored, in one way or another, until the noun is given.

The two different hypothesized strategies are depicted in Fig. 1.

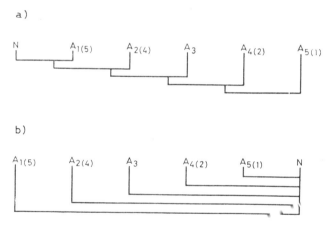

Fig. 1. Hypothesized decoding strategies for descriptions with noun first (a) and noun at the end (b).

The preceding description of decoding strategies are closely related to an earlier study of coding stations (Rommetveit and Turner, 1967). The problems are also connected to studies of word groups in encoding (Johnson, 1965), to models for speech encoding (Yngve, 1960), and to problems of "chunking" and "decision units" (Miller, 1962a, b, 1965).[1]

The delayed decoding suggested for conditions with noun at the end is in accordance with Uhlenbeck's principle of sustained memory (1963, p. 13) which holds that "a certain number of elements following one

1. The reader will probably also expect reference to studies of word groups in decoding using the click-technique (Fodor and Bever, 1965; Garrett, Bever and Fodor, 1966). After reading Larsen (1971), however, the author feels most uncertain about the interpretation of these studies and does not intend to include them here.

other linearly, may remain unconnected and kept present until an element or elements appearing in the utterance much later can be connected with them". This principle was first formulated by Stenzel and Reichling in the thirties (for references, see Uhlenbeck, 1963).

The difference between forms I and II, and the difference between forms III and IV, should not influence *the general strategy of decoding*, even though the different orders of adjectives may eventually affect the "final result of decoding", i.e. the actual impression formed of the secretary.

The expression "final result of decoding" may suggest that the meaning processes activated by the words in a description come to an end at a specific point in time. In an artificial experimental situation this may be so because of the nature of the stimulus material and because subsequent tasks might interrupt further processing. Such an abrupt ending of meaning processing will seldom be the case in ordinary communication, however. As emphasized in the discussion of the open and dynamic character of words, word meaning may be further enriched or modified by what is still to come.

4.2. The present experiments and the impression formation tradition

Since position of *adjectives* is varied in our experiments, they are relevant to a tradition of experiment on impression formation starting with Asch (1946). Asch's article "Forming impression of personality" refers to a series of experiments exploring how impressions of other persons are formed. Adjectives describing persons were always used as stimulus material. The task was ordinarily to form an impression of the kind of person described and to give a characterization of this person in a few sentences or through other methods.

The experiments by Asch have stimulated new research, and this is in particular true of experiment VI in his series. In the latter the following two series of adjectives were read to two different groups of college students, one series to each group.

A INTELLIGENT, INDUSTRIOUS, IMPULSIVE, CRITICAL, STUBBORN, ENVIOUS

B ENVIOUS, STUBBORN, CRITICAL, IMPULSIVE, INDUSTRIOUS, INTELLIGENT

Series A and B are identical with respect to words, but the order of the adjectives in B is the opposite of that in A. The subjects knew from the instruction that the list of words described a person, and their task was to form an impression of this person.

The purpose of this particular experiment was to explore whether it would be possible to alter the impression without changing any of the characteristics given. Such information would be crucial for deciding whether the total impression can be considered a sum of the impression of each word given separately. If simple, unweighted summation proved to be the answer, the order of adjectives should be of no importance; the impression formed on the basis of A should be identical to the one formed on the basis of B.

Asch reports, however, considerable differences between the two groups "taken as a whole". The impressions generated on the basis of A were more favourable than the impressions produced by B. In A, the most valuable characteristics are presented *first* in the description, while those traits come at the end of description B. When the description with the valuable characteristics *first* produce the most *favourable* impression, this means that the words heard first are in some way or another more important than words later in the series. This particular importance of the first elements is called a *primacy effect*.

Asch thus shows that *the order* of elements is of importance. He is not, however, the first to reach this conclusion. Order problems had earlier been investigated by Lund (25), although his "elements" and his interest were rather different from those of Asch. Lund had given a group of college students a mimeographed communication which supported one side of a controversial issue followed by a communication supporting the opposite view. The communication first presented seemed to influence the subjects much more than the communication given last, and on the basis of his results Lund formulated a law of primacy in persuasion.

Order problems in impression formation and persuasion have later been explored in a considerable number of studies. (Luchins, 1958; Anderson and Barrios, 1961; Anderson and Hubert, 1963; Anderson and Norman, 1964; Mayo and Crockett, 1964; Anderson, 1965; Stewart, 1965; Luchins, 1966a, b; Briscoe, Woodyard and Shaw, 1967; Anderson, 1968; Rosenbaum and Levin, 1968; McGinnis and Oziel, 1970; Margulis, Costanzo and Klein, 1971.) Hovland (1966) reports a number of studies devoted to explorations of order effects.

These studies have shown that a large number of factors influence which elements are given most importance. *Recency effects,* meaning that the elements last given are the most influential, are found as well as *primacy effects.* For a review of some of the relevant literature, see Jaspars (1966) and Jaspars *et al.* (1971).

In order to relate the present study more closely to earlier studies within the impression formation tradition, let us consider focal problems in some selected articles from this tradition and examine to what extent problems of communication are dealt with.

Asch (1946) does not explicitly deal with problems of communication although he uses *exclusively verbal stimulus material* in his experiments. He is clearly interested in the way we form impressions when encountering real persons and wants to generalize his results in this direction. This does not mean that Asch does not expect other processes also to be of importance in such cases. He is convinced, however, that the basic features he observed on the basis of his verbal material occur in the judgement of actual persons as well (Asch, 1946, p. 283).

Luchins (1958, 1966) uses *written* descriptions of a person in his investigations. He is much more explicitly concerned about this being a communication situation than is Asch. This is clearly revealed in the opening passage of his 1966 article (Luchins, 1966a, p. 33):

> The present investigation is concerned with evaluating the effects of various kinds and sequences of information communicated about an individual on the impressions formed concerning that person's personality and nature.

This means that the generalization of his results first of all is aimed at other situations where we form impressions of persons on the basis of *written* material. In the discussion parts of his articles, Luchins speculates on the implication of his results for impression formation of people in daily life, but is then more careful than Asch as far as generalization of results is concerned.

Anderson and Barrios seem to have a more general interest in communication, starting their presentation as follows (1961, p. 346): "Studies in communication research have reached no consensus as to the effect of order of presentation." In their experiments they use descriptions of persons composed of adjectives comparable to those used by Asch. Their choice of stimulus material, however, seems to be based upon practical considerations. They write (Anderson and Barrios, 1961,

p. 346): "The classic paper of Asch (1946) suggested the use of personality adjectives in order to get a large body of relatively homogenous material."

Both Luchins and Anderson and Barrios seem thus to be concerned with communication. In view of the expressed interest in communication we might expect that the impression formation process would be discussed in terms from the psychology of language and that the results would be related to other studies of language. This is not the case, however. In no case do they explore what their findings imply in terms of a theory of communication.

One additional special characteristic of the studies mentioned should also be noticed: In no case have the possibilities to vary the stimulus material been fully exploited. Anderson and Barrios inform their subjects in the instruction that a number of sets of adjectives will be presented and that each such set describes a person. What is varied is the number of adjectives and what might be called *the evaluative profile* of the description, that is, the special sequence of positive, negative or neutral adjectives. The stimulus material used by Luchins is descriptions of a person, Jim, formed in ordinary sentences. The stimulus material consists of an "introvert description" and "extrovert description" or of a combination of both.

What is varied is thus what roughly might be called the adjective part of the description. *It is important to notice that the subjects always have known at the moment any particular characteristic is given, what the latter refers to or what entity is being described.* As long as the guiding interest is how impressions are formed when meeting people in ordinary life, this must obviously be so: The actual concrete experience of human beauty or intelligence is always closely tied to a special person. We always know which person possesses the characteristic. But if *communication* is our primary research interest, this need not be so. It is possible to say: IT IS A LITTLE, COLD . . . before the listener gets to know what is referred to either through the verbal or non-verbal context.

The variation in the position of the noun then, giving: A SECRETARY WHO IS SEVERE, COOL, EXTRAORDINARY, BEAUTIFUL, PLEASANT and A SEVERE, COOL, EXTRAORDINARY, BEAUTIFUL, PLEASANT SECRETARY, represent a variation in the stimulus material which is of particular interest when we want to study communication.

4.3. What kind of data to use

What kind of data will yield significant information about differences in decoding depending on different word orders? In the following experiments, two sets of data have been used: (a) *Recall data*. Different words have been used as prompt words. The recall task as such was given after the subjects had listened to six descriptions, and the differences in recall between different conditions are in this case of particular importance. (b) *Impression formation data*. The subjects were simply asked how well they liked each entity immediately after the description was given. Again, differences between conditions are of primary importance.

What is the rationale for using these particular methods? We may first of all examine what the data will provide of information about *strategies of decoding*. Both memory data and data from the impression formation task contain such information. Knowledge about a resultant impression for instance, should contain clues to the processing leading up to it. The pertinent process is that of *decoding* or *understanding* which leads to a result which in this special case will be called *an impression*. Moreover, *retention* of this impression in long term memory is required in order to yield information about the impression later on when we try to assess what has been retained. This information can only be assessed via a process of *retrieval* and *re-encoding* on the part of the subject. This is only a very tentative outline of the sequence of processes that will be activated, however. In the condition where the noun is given after the series of adjectives, the "demarcation line" between memory processes and decoding seems to be rather unclear. The decoding strategies suggested for these cases imply that the adjectives have to be stored or remembered in one way or another. It may hence be argued that memory processes take place *before* as well as *after* the primary part of the decoding process, or it may be said that *decoding includes memory processes*. Choice between the two ways of describing the same composite processes seems to depend on in how broad or narrow a sense the term "decoding" is to be used. In this presentation we prefer to use decoding rather broadly, including all the different part-processes involved when the receiver understands what is being said or forms a fully-fledged impression of what has been described.

When talking about decoding as including memory processes and also being followed by memory processes, however, we must be open to the possibility that these memory processes most probably are of different

kinds. A more thorough discussion of the relation between memory pro
cesses and decoding strategies will be attempted in the discussion of the
results from the experiments.

4.3.1. RECALL DATA

Our data on recall are, more specifically, simply number of words given
back by the subjects when retrieval is prompted by one particular word.
If we just look at the way any one specific description is retained, it is
certainly different from the form in which it was originally presented to
the subject. In principle, the original description may have been transformed *during the decoding process, in memory,* or *in the final encoding.* Most
probably, retrieval performance will be affected by all of these processes,
and it is difficult to know which changes are due to which part process.
Is it possible, for example, that differences between conditions can be
fully explained by different retention processes only, i.e. by the memory
processes *following* the formation of impressions?

Although it is difficult to know exactly *where* in the chain decoding-
memory-encoding the observed changes take place, however, *a comparison* between results from different conditions may be revealing. If
descriptions of different forms via identical decoding strategies had
yielded similar impressions, how could the memorial processes make
them different? The "input" to memory would in such a case be identical and we would expect identical outcomes. Difference with respect to
retrieval presupposes some differences between initial impressions and
most probably also differences with respect to decoding. Differences in
impression, however, may activate somewhat different memorial processes which in turn may aggravate or diminish already established differences. In addition, differences with respect to encoding mechanisms
may also influence the final retrieval outcome.

Potential differences in encoding may in principle be traced back to
different factors. First, differences in memory may explain the differences. An example of this would be that the subjects actually make use
of different standards of certainty before *reporting* words under different
conditions. If they feel that their performance is below some internal
standard, they may for instance tend to fill in more words, and such a
strategy may be felt to be necessary only under particular conditions.

In addition, encoding strategies may be controlled by external factors
such as, for example, the instruction and other experimentally induced

conditions for recall. In the present experiment *the same instructions and conditions* have been used in connection with descriptions of different forms. This possible source of variance has thus been eliminated. In one variant of the experiment, however, recall was prompted by two different words, both words being used across different forms of the description. This yields in addition a possibility to examine the results of one possible change in encoding conditions.

Our first conclusion then, is that differences revealed in retrieval imply differences in *impressions* and *decoding*. It is difficult to know, however, how memorial and encoding processes enter the picture.

Some of the problems we encounter resemble those encountered in an experiment by Rommetveit and Turner (1967). The latter found differences in retention between descriptions such as

(A) A LEFTWARD, JAGGEDLY DESCENDING, BROKEN CURVE

and

(B) A JAGGED, BROKEN CURVE DESCENDING LEFTWARD

with version A leading to the best retention. Both of the words LEFTWARD and DESCENDING were, for example, retained by 14 out of 27 subjects in the A-condition, but only by two out of 28 subjects in the B-condition. CURVE was used as prompt word in this recall task.

Following our conclusion above, such differences in recall imply differences with respect to impressions (or messages, as Rommetveit and Turner call it) and decoding, and Rommetveit and Turner also try to explain these differences by hypothesizing different decoding strategies for version A and B.

In view of what has been said about the possibility of interaction between message and memory processes, this may be as far as we may reach with recall data. An explanation in terms of a reference to some difference without specifying precisely how the two decoding strategies differ, seems rather unsatisfactory, and Rommetveit and Turner's explanation is further elaborated in the decoding strategies depicted in Fig. 2.

These hypothesized strategies are consistent with the results of the recall task for the following reason: In B the first four words form a word group. DESCENDING and LEFTWARD are tied onto this group and *not* to CURVE directly. It is therefore reasonable that DESCENDING and LEFTWARD very seldom are given back when CURVE is used as prompt word. In condition A, on the other hand, every word is tied directly onto CURVE, which therefore functions much better as a prompt word for DESCENDING and LEFTWARD.[1] This is in brief, the explanation offered by Rommetveit and Turner.

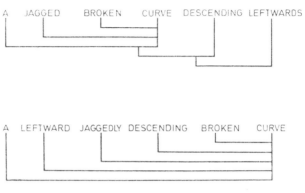

Fig. 2. Two hypothesized decoding strategies.

It is claimed that Fig. 2 depicts decoding strategies, but it might just as well be interpreted as depicting *the structure of the received message.* This points to a problem concerning the relationship between processing and the structure of cross-cuts at specific points in time. In the case of Rommetveit and Turner, this problem is not explicitly discussed, but a rather simple and direct relationship between processing and "final" result seems to be presupposed. Let us hence for the clarity of exposition interpret Fig. 2 as depicting the structure of the received message. *The latter is portrayed in some pattern of connections or ties between words or wordgroups, a pattern that it seems reasonable to test by some sort of retention measurement.* The specific character of these connections is not known, but most probably they must be of a more complicated character than simple associations. Some connections may thus possibly have the character of one element serving as a presupposition or background for another. To such questions we will return later.

1. One possible way to check this explanation could be to use the word group A JAGGED, BROKEN CURVE as prompt words. These prompt words should function better as a prompt for DESCENDING in condition B than in condition A. In the figure DESCENDING is assigned a direct connection to the whole word group in the former condition, whereas this is not the case in the latter condition.

Despite this uncertainty, we may safely assume that closely connected words will be more resistant to later interference and give superior recall. In the present experiment, six different descriptions were presented successively, and recall was not required until all six descriptions had been presented. The set of descriptions functions as interfering material, and this obviously very unusual context has the effect of really putting to test the different sorts of connections existing within a description. According to the above view, then, the task of retention does not only enter as noise, but may actually function as some sort of *test of the cohesion* of the different parts.

Resort to data on memory processes in the study of language structures may appear as a detour. In the case of Rommetveit and Turner as well as in the following experiments, however, recall tasks seem reasonable. The only presupposition regarding memory inherent in our argument is that words most closely connected in decoding and final impression will be those most resistant to interference.

A comparison between descriptions with the same *form*, but composed of different *words*, may also be revealing. The final impressions ought in that case to have *the same structure*, and potential differences with respect to recall would have to be explained in terms of, e.g. different aspects of semantic-associative networks. The basis for our inference from retrieval to decoding strategy, however, will be descriptions with *different form* but composed of the *same words*. Semantic competence thus should affect retrieval in the same way across different conditions.

The discussion above is closely related to Fillenbaum's (1970, 1973) discussion of the use of direct as compared to indirect methods involving memory processes in the study of syntactic structures. It also reminds us of the problem of *qualitative changes* in memory and whether they take place in the perceptual phase, the memory phase, or in the retrieval phase (Kvale, 1974a).

4.3.2. IMPRESSION FORMATION DATA

The specific data on impression formation are simply the positions of checkmarks on a scale for every description by every subject. Before discussing what sort of information can be gained by such means, one specific function of an impression formation setting should be noted. When the subjects are asked to form impressions of what is being described and to communicate this impression by checkmarks, they are forced to attend to *the meaning* of the descriptions. If there had been a request for recall data only, undue attention might have been paid to word *forms*. Experimental language processing would, if that were the case, deviate from ordinary language usage. The use of memory techniques in the study of language structure has been questioned because of this possibility of a rather special and artificially induced form of language processing by Rommetveit and Turner (1967) and Fillenbaum (1970, 1973). If memory techniques are used, they should include some sort of task presupposing focus on meaning. In the present case, the impression formation task serves this function.

The subjects in our tasks were asked to place the checkmarks according to how they liked what was described, and their checkmarks should thus convey rather direct information about at least one aspect of the impression. Mere knowledge of how positive subjects judge a certain thing or person to be, however, does not seem to be of particular interest in itself. *Differences* between conditions, however, may be revealing for its own sake and as potential clues to different decoding strategies.

4.3.3. NOTES ON POSSIBLE RELATIONSHIPS BETWEEN RECALL DATA AND IMPRESSION FORMATION DATA

Both recall and impression formation data are thus generated in the present experiments. Different *relationships* may hold between these two sets of data. One particularly significant factor in this context pertains to the distinction between *intentional* and *incidental* recall. This distinction is used in accordance with Postman's (1968) suggestion to differentiate between tasks where the instructions prepare the subjects for the recall task to come and tasks where no prior warning of such task is given. The experimental part of the monograph contains two main experiments, Experiment I and Experiment II, and the main difference between the two is precisely the difference between intentional and incidental recall. In Experiment I, the subjects were informed about both the impression formation task and the recall task in the initial instruction. In Experiment II, on the other hand, the task was introduced simply as impression formation. The recall task was introduced without prior warning afterwards, when the impression formation part had been fulfilled. What, then, is our reason for studying both intentional and incidental recall?

Postman (1968) maintains that the results of intentional as compared to incidental learning depends upon the relationship between the learning task and what he calls the orienting task, that is, the task used (Postman, 1968, p. 188) "to ensure the exposure of S to the learning material". In other words: the relationship between the results from an intentional and an incidental task, is dependent on the kind of strategies adopted. Conversely, then, a comparison between intentional and incidental recall should in the present case provide clues with respect to which strategy of decoding is employed. The impression formation task will in this connection function as an orienting task.

Such a rationale is admittedly rather vague. But even exploratory approaches may be revealing at present since so little systematic knowledge of the relationship between language processing and memory processes has been established. It should also be noted that Fillenbaum (1973) in a discussion of models of human memory and memory for sentences tries to direct workers in psycholinguistics towards the distinction between intentional and incidental learning. The latter has so far primarily been emphasized within studies of verbal learning and memory.

4.4. Two experiments exploring effects of noun position

Two earlier experiments exploring effects of noun position will be discussed in this section. The first is an experiment by Lambert and Paivio (1956) and the second is the experiment by Rommetveit and Turner earlier referred to (p. 65). The results of these experiments are of interest in themselves. Both of the studies differ, however, in important respects from the present one, and we intend to point out these differences and argue for our particular choice of experimental procedure.

Lambert and Paivio (1956) employed a learning approach with several presentations of the stimulus material in their study. Two lists of words each composed of 28 words, were presented to the subjects. The words in the lists were in groups of four, indicated by a somewhat longer pause after every fourth word. The structure within these groups differed from one list to another. In one case a noun was always the first word followed by three appropriate adjectives. In the other case the noun was the last word in the group. The subjects were not informed about the nature of the words to be presented. Their task was only to learn the lists to the criterion of two errorless runs by an anticipation method.

The result shows that the mean number of trials required to reach this criterion was significantly lower when the noun had been the first word in the group. In this study the task required the noun to be remembered as well as the adjectives. The recall of adjectives *per se*, however, was also more difficult in lists with the noun at the end of each subpart. More errors were made before the adjectives were learned in this case.

Lambert and Paivio's learning approach with several presentations of the stimulus material is clearly in contrast to the single presentation of stimulus material in the present study. For an understanding of normal communication, data from studies using single presentation are of more direct relevance. The learning approach differs, moreover, from the combined impression formation and recall task given to the subjects in the present experiments. The former approach may imply a too heavy emphasis upon retention. The latter approach, though clearly artificial, is more close to ordinary communication in that the impression formation task requires the subjects to focus on meaning.

In the study by Rommetveit and Turner (1967) the subjects were asked to remember descriptions like A LEFTWARD, JAGGEDLY DESCENDING, BROKEN CURVE and A JAGGED, BROKEN CURVE DESCENDING LEFTWARD. It was observed that LEFTWARD and DESCENDING were much better recalled when presented in pre-position to the noun than when presented in post-position.

There are several differences between the Rommetveit and Turner study and the present one. In the present study, the adjectives function as *attributes or predicate words*. In the study by Rommetveit and Turner, adjective-noun combinations represented relationships of *apposition* as well as of *attribution* (*ibid.* p. 351). DESCENDING LEFTWARD may even function as a *verb phrase* when it comes after the noun (*ibid.* p. 349). Such formally defined differences are confounded with *functional similarity* in the actual experimental situation, however. The subjects were to identify the described curve among many similar curves drawn on a paper. In order to identify the correct curve, each characteristic would accordingly be of equal importance. Functional similarity may have overridden the more abstract structural differences, but the confounding of these aspects complicates the interpretation of results. The stimulus material used in our experiments is from such a point of view much simpler in that the adjectives always function as attributes or predicate words.

Another difference between the two studies is perhaps more important, however. It was argued that decoding of adjectives in Noun-end descriptions has to be postponed because it remains uncertain precisely *what* these adjectives refer to until the noun is given. In the case of Rommetveit and Turner, care was taken *to reduce the ambiguity of each adjective in advance (ibid.* p. 345): "Each of the descriptive adjectives was explained to the subject and/or explicated by simple visual demonstration prior to the experimental task". In contrast, care has been taken to secure that the adjectives should remain open and yet not fully determined until the noun is presented in the present experiments. For explorations of decoding in Noun-end conditions, the latter procedure seems preferable. Uncertainty as to reference of some of the words involved, seems to be one of the main and special characteristics of such situations and should thus also characterize the experimental set up.

4.5. Summary of Rationale for design

We investigate here how decoding strategies depend on the sequence in which words are presented. One main difference as to order in normal communication situations, is the difference between pre-position versus post-position of topic. This variation is exemplified in the stimulus material by use of *Noun-first* versus *Noun-end* descriptions. The same variation is involved also in other studies (Lambert and Paivio, 1956; Rommetveit and Turner, 1967). The task there given, however, have characteristics which make the generalization of results to more normal communication situations questionable.

The experimental task in the present study is one of impression formation and recall. In the impression formation tradition sequence problems have often been explored by *variation in adjective sequences*. The latter variable is also adopted here because possible effects on impressions may give clues to the way in which the information is processed. The impression formation task has in addition been included to secure processing of meaning.

In the exploration of decoding strategies one aim is to illuminate "connections" or "relations" between words and it is argued that a postponed recall task with intervening and interfering material may yield information of relevance. Information about "connections" may also be provided by the use of different prompt words, and both *noun and first adjective* are used to prompt recall.

The experiments also includes the variation between *intentional and incidental recall*. This variation is included because the relationship between data from these two types of situations may provide additional information about the strategies employed.

4.6. Expectations concerning results

As far as results are concerned, we have few specific expectations, and arguments could in many cases be given for just opposite outcomes.

Regarding recall performance it might be argued that more adjectives should be recalled when the noun is given at the end of the description than when it occurs in first position, provided that the *noun* is given as prompt word. This expectation is based on the two hypothesized decoding strategies depicted in Fig. 1, given that these figures are interpreted rather "literally" such that the lines are interpreted as connections existing between the words.

If so, the figure depicting descriptions with noun first shows that *only the first adjective is connected directly to the noun*. Every other adjective is connected to a noun already modified by preceding adjectives. The noun might hence be expected to be a good prompt word for the first adjective, but not for the later. For descriptions with the noun at the end, on the other hand, the figure seems to imply direct connections from the noun to every adjective. Consequently, the noun should be an excellent prompt word for every adjective. Such reasoning would lead us to predict best recall of adjectives in the cases where the noun was given at the end of the description.

But we may also argue for just the opposite kind of relationship between recall data in Noun-first and Noun-end descriptions, that is, for superior recall when the noun is given in first position. Such a prediction follows from different opportunities for integration in the two cases, and it takes as a presupposition that integration facilitates recall. When the noun is given in first position, the information conveyed by each adjective can be integrated with what at each stage has been made known already in a cumulative fashion. This means that the total time available for integration includes both the time it takes to present each description and the time passing until the next description is heard. When the noun is given in last position, on the other hand, integration must be achieved mainly within the interval between two descriptions. That is, less time is available for integration in Noun-end descriptions than in Noun-first descriptions, and we may accordingly expect best recall in the latter case.

The two studies exploring effects of noun position discussed in the previous section appear, furthermore, to point in different directions. In the study by Rommetveit and Turner (1967), pre-position of words yielded best recall, whereas Lambert and Paivio (1956) demonstrated superior recall with noun in first position. A point of view rather similar to the one here advocated when it was argued for superior recall for Noun-first descriptions, is actually adopted in the latter study in the discussion of results (*ibid.* p. 12): 'The relatedness of group members is determined by the noun, relatedness is high when the noun appears early and low when the noun appears late."

The tasks given to the subjects in the two studies discussed, moreover, differ so much in theoretically important respects from those given in the present experiments that it seems at present highly questionable to use their data as a basis for firm predictions concerning recall. Our experimental set-up will hopefully, however, provide information of relevance for further discussions of the importance of such differences for recall in Noun-first as compared to Noun-end situations.

As regards the impression formation data, we have one specified expectation. When the noun is given in first position and no instruction for recall is added to the task of impression formation, the task seems to be rather similar to those in the impression formation tradition ordinarily giving primacy effects (for example: Asch, 1946; Anderson and Barrios, 1961; Anderson and Hubert, 1963; Luchins, 1966a; McGinnis and Oziel, 1970). We should hence expect a primacy effect in this case. When the subjects have been prepared for the recall task before they form their impressions, more uncertainty arises. Anderson and Hubert (1963) included a condition in which subjects were informed both of the impression formation task and the recall task in the initial instruction. In this case, a weak recency effect was obtained. *The timing of the recall task* differs between their study and the present, however. In the former, recall of a given description was requested immediately after the subjects had formed their impressions of that specific description. In the present study, on the other hand, recall is postponed until the subjects have formed impressions of each of the six descriptions. The timing of recall may very well affect the strategies chosen by the subjects and thus also the order effects to be obtained.

As for order effects pertaining to descriptions with noun at the end, nothing is known from other studies. If we interpret Fig. 1 literally, we may argue that there is a moment at which every adjective is attended to simultaneously with the noun. One peculiar implication would then be that order as such would be of negligible importance in this case. Such a prediction, however, goes contrary to what has earlier been claimed concerning the importance of temporal sequence in language.

Rommetveit (1968, p. 280) has suggested that the primacy effect often observed in impression formation may be explained in terms of pragmatic notions. What is first said is as a rule that which is of greatest importance. Conversely, what is said last is of least importance and borders on what is so unimportant as not to be mentioned at all. If so— and provided that the decoding is on the speaker's premises—a primacy effect might be expected for Noun-end descriptions as well as for Noun-first descriptions.

Once more, however, arguments may also be offered for the opposite expectation, that is, for recency. At the moment when the noun is heard, the adjective presented immediately before it will have the advantage of being more salient, and a recency effect would hence occur.

Thus, we have few precise predictions, and the final design aims primarily at *diagnosis*. It aims at a systematic combination of experimental conditions by which we hope to illuminate unresolved issues concerning temporal sequence and decoding strategies in previous research.

5

The Main Experiments
Experiments I and II

5.1. Design and procedure of Experiment I and Experiment II

In what follows, design and procedure of the two main experiments in this monograph will be reported. Experiment I will be described in some detail. Experiment II is very similar to Experiment I and only the differences between them will be described. The two experiments are in fact so closely related that they may be considered different conditions of one main experiment.

5.1.1. DESIGN AND PROCEDURE OF EXPERIMENT I

Six descriptions of the following form were used as stimulus material in the experiment: A SECRETARY WHO IS SEVERE, COOL, EXTRAORDINARY, BEAUTIFUL, PLEASANT. (The construction of descriptions will be further explained on p. 80.)

There were four experimental conditions in a 2×2 design. The two experimental variables were *Noun position* (Noun-first versus Noun-end) and *Order of adjectives* (A_1-A_5) and (A_5-A_1). The conditions are labelled

TABLE 1

Design of experiment I

	A_1-A_5	A_5-A_1
Noun-first	I	II
Noun-end	III	IV

I, II, III, IV. For the relationships between these labels and the experimental variables, see Table 1.

The subjects were tested in groups, one group for every condition. Instructions and the stimulus material were presented by means of a tape-recorder. Every subject was given a pencil and a small booklet. The instruction was as follows:

You are now to take part in a small study of how one forms impressions when hearing descriptions of things, happenings and people, and how well one remembers them shortly after.

I shall read you six unconnected descriptions. All have the same form as the one I am now about to read:
A STORY WHICH IS SAD, UNPLEASANT, DIRTY, ORIGINAL, LONG (Conditions I and II)
A SAD, UNPLEASANT, DIRTY, ORIGINAL, LONG STORY (Conditions III and IV).

Your task is, after each description, to form an immediate impression as to how you like what is described. If you turn to page 2 in your booklet, you will find 7 squares with different headings. You are to show your immediate impression by putting a check-mark in the square with the heading which coincides most with your impression. To make quite sure that you express your immediate impression, you will be given only 4 seconds to make a check-mark for every description. As soon as you have made a mark, you are to turn to the next page, so that you are ready for the next description.
When all the descriptions have been read aloud you are to recall them by writing down what you remember of them.

We shall run through 2 examples before we start on the experiment proper. Listen carefully. Form your impression quickly and mark the appropriate square. Then, turn to the next page.

A FRIEND WHO IS DARING, COMPLICATED, ENCOURAGING, WARM, KIND (Conditions I and II)

A DARING, COMPLICATED, ENCOURAGING, WARM, KIND FRIEND (Conditions III and IV)

[4 seconds pause]

A SCULPTURE WHICH IS POWERFUL, HEAVY, ROUND, CAPTIVATING, HARMONIOUS (Conditions I and II)

A POWERFUL, HEAVY, ROUND, CAPTIVATING, HARMONIOUS SCULPTURE (Conditions III and IV)

[4 seconds pause]

On the following two pages there is room to write down the descriptions you have heard. (Here the nouns of the descriptions were used as prompt words in the sequence SCULPTURE—FRIEND). The order of the adjectives used is of no importance. Just write down all the words you remember. If you feel uncertain about some of the words, not being quite sure that they are correct, write down those too. Work as fast as you can. And—one more thing—you must not look back to previous pages. Please begin.

[Pause—until most of the subjects had fulfilled the recall task.]

You have perhaps already noticed that the order of descriptions is different when I read them aloud and when you write them down according to what you remember. This will also be the case in the main experiment. If anyone has not understood what is to be done, raise your hand. Your questions will be answered individually.

[Pause for possible questions and answers.]

Then we shall begin. When all 6 descriptions have been read aloud and you have made your check-marks, just continue with the memory task. Listen carefully.

A SECRETARY WHO IS SEVERE, COOL, EXTRAORDINARY, BEAUTIFUL, PLEASANT (Condition I, noun first, A_1–A_5).

Five more descriptions describing A CHAIR, A MOVIE, AN ACTRESS, A FARMER and A BOOK were given in the order above with a pause of four seconds between descriptions.

In the small booklets, the first four pages were used for the examples, the two first of these for the impression task, the two last for the recall task. On the pages to be used in the former task there were seven small squares composing a scale. Each square had a verbal label, or heading, written above: Extremely bad, Very bad, Bad, Medium, Good, Very good, Extremely good.

On the page for the recall task, part of the description was given as prompt with clearly marked places for the words to be filled in (cf. the following examples).

A sculpture which is — — — — — — — — — — — — — —
(Conditions I and II)

A — — — — — — — — — — — — — — — — — sculpture
(Conditions III and IV)

The pages to be used in the experiment proper were organized in the same way. First, there were six pages to be used to report impression formation followed by six pages for recall. Retrieval was requested in the following sequence: ACTRESS, MOVIE, FARMER, CHAIR, BOOK, SECRETARY.

5.1.2. DESIGN AND PROCEDURE OF EXPERIMENT II

In this experiment there were eight experimental conditions in a $2 \times 2 \times 2$ design. The three experimental variables were *Noun position* (Noun-first versus Noun-end), *Order of adjectives* (A_1–A_5 verus A_5–A_1), and *Kind of prompt word* (Noun as prompt word versus first adjective as prompt word). The adjective used as a prompt word was always the one first presented. In Noun-first conditions, therefore, the adjective *closest to the noun* was used as a prompt word, whereas in Noun-end conditions, the prompt word was the adjective *furthest away from the noun.*

The different conditions are labelled I_N, I_A, II_N, II_A, III_N, III_A, IV_N, IV_A. For the relationship between these labels and the experimental variables, see Table 2.

TABLE 2

Design of experiment II

	A_1–A_5	A_5–A_1
	Noun prompt I_N	Noun prompt II_N
Noun-first		
	I_A Adjective prompt	II_A Adjective prompt
	Noun prompt III_N	Noun prompt IV_N
Noun-end		
	III_A Adjective prompt	IV_A Adjective prompt

The procedure of Experiment II was essentially the same as that of Experiment I, except for the fact that the recall task was given after the impression formation task *without any prior warning*.

The only changes made in instruction and booklets of Experiment I, was to take out every hint of the recall task. When the subjects had finished the impression formation task, they were given another small booklet for the recall test. The instruction for recall was as follows:

> You were not asked to remember the descriptions you were read, but some of you remember perhaps parts of them anyway. In the booklet just given you, there is room to write down whatever you might remember of the descriptions. On each page in the booklet, a prompt word is given. Your task is to try to fill in the rest of the description this word is taken from. On the first page in the booklet you will find an example of how this is to be done. The order of the words is of no importance. Just write down all the words you remember. If you feel uncertain about some of the words, not being quite sure that they are correct, write down these too. And one more thing—you must never look back to the previous pages. Work as fast as you can. Please begin.

The six descriptions used in Experiment I were again used as stimulus material. They were given in exactly the same form as in the previous experiment by just playing them over to the new magnetic-tape.

When the first adjective was used as prompt word, the noun had also to be recalled. This was shown by the example presented first in the recall booklet.

5.2. Subjects in Experiment I and Experiment II

Twenty subjects, 10 male and 10 female, participated in every condition of Experiment I, giving a total of 80 subjects. The subjects were mostly students taking a combined course in logic, psychology, and philosophy serving as an obligatory introduction to further studies for all students. In order to attain the required 20 subjects in every condition, however, some subjects from a rather similar student population were recruited. These were first year's students of psychology. The subjects were run in groups, one group for every condition. Their average age varied between 19 years 9 months, and 22 years 11 months in the different conditions.

Twenty subjects, 10 male and 10 female, also participated in every condition of Experiment II, giving a total of 160 subjects. The subjects were again run in groups, one group for every condition.

They were also students taking their obligatory course in logic, psychology and philosophy, and their average age varied between 19 years 4 months and 20 years 1 month in the different conditions.

5.3. The stimulus material

5.3.1. THE DESCRIPTIONS

The stimulus material consisted of the following six descriptions. As the experiments were conducted in Norwegian, each description is given both in Norwegian and in English translation.

1. A SECRETARY WHO IS SEVERE, COOL, EXTRA-ORDINARY, BEAUTIFUL, PLEASANT.
   (EN SEKRETÆR SOM ER STRENG, KJØLIG, UVANLIG, SKJØNN, BEHAGELIG.)
2. A CHAIR WHICH IS SOFT, TALL, GREY, DREARY, UGLY
   (EN STOL SOM ER MYK, HØY, GRÅ, TRIST, STYGG)
3. A MOVIE WHICH IS SPOILT, DISGUSTING, PECULIAR, DEMANDING, IMPORTANT
   (EN FILM SOM ER ØDELAGT, VEMMELIG, MERKELIG, KREVENDE, BETYDNINGSFULL)
4. AN ACTRESS WHO IS VERSATILE, EXCITING, LOVELY, PURE, DECEPTIVE
   (EN SKUESPILLERINNE SOM ER MANGFOLDIG, SPEN-NENDE, VAKKER, REN, LUMSK)
5. A FARMER WHO IS THICK, OLD, DARK, ATTRACTIVE, FRIENDLY
   (EN BONDE SOM ER TETT, GAMMEL, MØRK, TILTREK-KENDE, VENNLIG)
6. A BOOK WHICH IS LARGE, BROWN, GLOOMY, UN-IMAGINATIVE, DISORGANIZED
   (EN BOK SOM ER STOR, BRUN, DYSTER, FANTASILØS, ROTETE)

Each description consists of a noun (N) followed by five adjectives (A's). Three of the nouns belong to the class of "persons", whereas the remaining three belong to the class of "things". In the experiments, these descriptions were used exactly in the form given above (Condition

I), with the order of adjectives reversed (Condition II), or with the noun following each one of the different sequences of adjectives (Conditions III and IV).[1] (See p 52 for the description of SECRETARY in its four possible forms.) In addition to these six descriptions the following three were used as examples:

7. A STORY WHICH IS SAD, UNPLEASANT, DIRTY, ORIGINAL, LONG
   (EN HISTORIE SOM ER TRIST, UBEHAGELIG, SKITTEN, ORIGINAL, LANG)
8. A FRIEND WHO IS DARING, COMPLICATED, ENCOURAGING, WARM, KIND
   (EN VENN SOM ER DRISTIG, KOMPLISERT, OPPMUNTRENDE, VARM, GOD)
9. A SCULPTURE WHICH IS POWERFUL, HEAVY, ROUND, CAPTIVATING, HARMONIOUS
   (EN SKULPTUR SOM ER KRAFTIG, TUNG, RUND, FENGSLENDE, HARMONISK)

Our construction of descriptions was largely based upon intuition, but yet in accordance with a superordinate rationale. An attempt will now be made to summarize the principles guiding the construction. The following considerations, however, will only be of immediate relevance for *the original Norwegian version* since important semantic characteristics necessarily are modified in the translation.

In the construction of stimulus material, one special consideration was of primary importance: The combination of adjectives within a description should not severely restrict the possibilities with respect to *what kinds of noun might follow*. Absence of such constraints are prerequisites for different decoding strategies in the case where the noun comes ahead of, as compared to at the end of, the series of adjectives. If one special combination of adjectives strongly suggests the relevant noun, the decoding strategy adopted for descriptions with the noun at the end may be rather similar to the one employed in response to descriptions with the noun first. Leading combinations of adjectives may thus minimize expected differences between possible strategies, and each noun should hence be non-redundant, though

1. Condition I (II, III, IV) refers in this connection to Condition I (II, III, IV) in Experiment I and Conditions I_N (II_N, III_N, IV_N) and I_A (II_A, III_A, IV_A) in Experiment II. For simplicity, the symbols for the conditions are used in this way throughout the part describing the stimulus material.

still reasonable, when appearing at the end of the description. Those combinations reducing possibilities minimally, however, may create problems of their own. Such combinations will tend to be of a rather unusual kind and thereby make it difficult to generalize to verbal communication in ordinary life. The possibilities of forming impressions, on the basis of too peculiar combinations may also be questioned.

Such were the considerations. To check for redundancy inherent in the descriptions, moreover, 16 subjects were given the combinations of adjectives in written form and asked to write down the first *thing*, *happening* or *person* these adjectives made them think of. Details and results are given in Appendix A. The results show that the range of possible nouns was more restricted in the case of the adjective combinations referring to persons (SECRETARY, ACTRESS, FARMER) than for the rest of the descriptions (CHAIR, MOVIE, BOOK). In the latter case, almost none of the answers came close to the actual nouns. This difference between the two sets of nouns, must be kept in mind in the subsequent discussion of our data.

In addition to the attempt to make the combination of adjectives open-ended with respect to what sort of entity they might describe, we also tried to ensure such an openness by the way of instruction. Three examples were used in the instruction, a description of a STORY, a FRIEND and a SCULPTURE. These introductory examples should make for uncertainty with respect to which kinds of entities might be expected.

Another principle guiding the construction was that the adjectives within each description should differ with respect to how positive or negative they would be judged to be. Changes in the evaluative score of impressions due to reversal of the sequence of adjectives, depend on such characteristics of the descriptions.

In practice, this principle was followed by inserting two adjectives which we judged to be positive independent of their context in three of the descriptions, and two adjectives which we judged to be negative independent of context in the last three of the descriptions.[1] The rest of

1. It should be noticed that the three descriptions with the positive adjectives are the descriptions of "persons", while the three descriptions with negative adjectives are those describing "things". This is the result of a pretest where subjects were ask to mark natural and unnatural descriptions. The combination of adjectives including the two positive ones were then judged to be more naturally followed by a person than by a thing, whereas the result was the reverse for combinations including the negative adjectives.

the adjectives within the sets were chosen with less constraints, but in such a way that the adjectives within a set most probably would vary on an evaluative scale.

The sequence of adjectives within a given set was decided by a rather special procedure used to assess what might be called a "natural order". Fourteen subjects were asked to arrange the five adjectives in the order which seemed most natural when characterizing the special noun used in the description. The "natural order" was then defined in terms of the outcome of this pretest. For details, see Appendix B.

This procedure made it a matter of chance what sort of "evaluative profile" the descriptions would have. It turn out somewhat surprisingly, however, that the adjectives were "naturally ordered" rather regularly with the most positive adjectives first and the most negative ones last. This conclusion is supported by the results of a rather informal rating of the adjectives by eight colleagues of the author. For results of this rating procedure, see Appendix C.

In the actual experiment, possible effects of "natural sequence" of adjectives is controlled for. CHAIR, ACTRESS and BOOK are presented with "natural sequence" of adjectives in Conditions I and III, while SECRETARY, MOVIE and FARMER are presented with the adjectives in opposite order. For Conditions II and IV the sequences are reversed.

5.3.2. THE TECHNICAL PRODUCTION OF THE STIMULUS MATERIAL

As mentioned earlier, the material was presented by a tape-recorder. To prevent different patterns of intonation or pauses, the adjective parts of the description were identical in Conditions I (N A_1–A_5) and III (A_1–A_5 N) as well as in Conditions II (N A_5–A_1) and IV (A_5–A_1 N). This was obtained by first making a master tape where every description was read in the following form: A SECRETARY WHO IS SEVERE, COOL, EXTRAORDINARY, BEAUTIFUL, PLEAS-ANT SECRETARY. For Condition I the last SECRETARY was cut out when playing the material on to a second tape, for Condition III the first SECRETARY WHO IS was left out.

An identical procedure was used to make the adjective part of Conditions II (N A_5–A_1) and IV (A_5–A_1 N) identical. In order also to keep these conditions close to Conditions I and III, efforts were made to read the five adjectives comparably rapid in both orders. (The time to read the five adjectives varied from 7·5 to 10 seconds for the different descriptions). A stop-watch was used to measure time all through these experiments. Thus, only crude measurements were applied.

The instruction was also read on the master tape and then played onto the tapes of the different conditions. Only the examples had to be different in *Noun-first* and *Noun-end* conditions.

6

The Results of Experiments I and II

6.1. Results from the recall tasks

A short summary of the main results from the recall tasks will first be given.

1. The recall of adjectives is about twice as good in Noun-first as in Noun-end conditions.
2. The warning that a recall task will follow influences recall in Noun-first conditions, but not in Noun-end conditions. That is, intentional recall is superior to incidental recall in Noun-first conditions, but not in Noun-end conditions.
3. The recall of an adjective is much more dependent on the position of that adjective in Noun-end than in Noun-first conditions.
4. The difference between number of adjectives tagged onto correct noun and total number of adjectives recalled is much greater in Noun-end than in Noun-first conditions.
5. When the first adjective is used as prompt word, recall of the remaining adjectives is much poorer than when the noun serves as the prompt word.
6. In cases where first adjective is used as prompt word recall of the noun is much better than the recall of the adjectives within the description.
7. When a wrong noun is reproduced in response to an adjective prompt word, more of the adjectives recalled are connected to that incorrect noun than to the prompt word.

6.1.1 NOUN-FIRST VERSUS NOUN-END

Total recall

Recall is superior in Noun-first conditions. This is shown in Figs. 3 and 4 comparing the average number of adjectives given back to correct noun in Noun-first and Noun-end conditions in Experiment I and Experiment II respectively. (Tables giving average numbers are found in Appendix D, Tables D1 and D2. In these tables the results are also split up for adjective order $A_1–A_5$ versus $A_5–A_1$.)

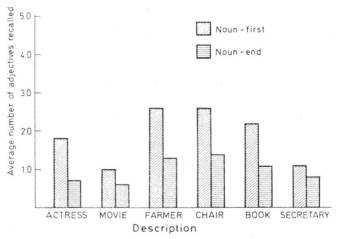

Fig. 3. Average number of adjectives recalled to each noun. Experiment I.

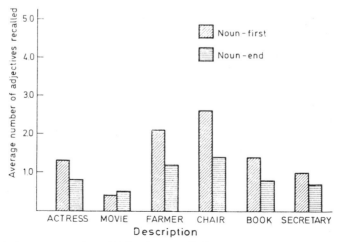

Fig. 4. Average number of adjectives recalled to each noun. Experiment II.

Figure 3 shows that recall of adjectives was superior in Noun-first conditions for every description in Experiment I. About twice as many adjectives were recalled in this case (11·3) as compared to Noun-end conditions (5·7).

Figure 4 shows that the same general outcome is replicated in Experiment II. For every description except MOVIE, recall of adjectives was superior in Noun-first conditions. The averages for Noun-first and Noun-end conditions were in this case 8·7 and 5·4 respectively.

An analysis of variance (see Table 3) shows that the effect of position of the noun is significant at $p < 0.001$.

TABLE 3

Analysis of variance of data from Experiments I and II. Noun as prompt word. Every adjective given back to correct noun is counted as correct.

Source	Sum of squares	df	Estimate	F	p
N	805·51	1	805·51	90·10	0·001
In	79·81	1	79·81	8·93	0·01
A	17·56	1	17·56	1·96	
Within cells	1358·95	152	8·94		
N × In	48·88	1	48·88	5·47	0·05
N × A	13·81	1	13·81	1·54	
In × A	1·81	1	1·81	0·20	
N × In × A	18·18	1	18·18	2·03	

N: Noun position
In: Instruction
A: Adjective sequence

Figures 3 and 4 also show that the six descriptions differ with respect to ease of recall. The adjectives connected to CHAIR have been recalled most frequently, whereas the adjectives connected to MOVIE show poorest recall. The effect of description (D) is significant with $p < 0.001$, $p < 0.05$, $p < 0.05$, $p < 0.01$ according to the analyses of variance summarized in Table 4, p. 88. It must be noted, however, that only recall data for positions 1 and 5 are included in these analyses.

Instruction

As expected, subjects recall more adjectives in Experiment I than in Experiment II, the effect of instruction being significant at $p < 0.01$

(Table 3). The most interesting result, however, seems to be the significant interaction between type of instruction and position of noun.

TABLE 4

A summary of significant effects found in 4 analyses of variance performed on recall data for position 1 and position 5.

Source	Experiment I		Experiment II	
	Men	Women	Men	Women
N	0·01	0·01		0·05
A				0·05
NA	0·05			
S:NA		0·01		
D	0·001	0·05	0·05	0·01
DN				0·05
DA	0·01			
DNA		0·01		
DS:NA			≈0·05	
P				
PN	0·05	0·01		
PA				
PNA			0·05	
PS:NA				
DP				
DPN				
DPA	0·01	0·001	0·001	0·01
DPAN				
DPS:NA				

N: Noun position
A: Adjective sequence
S: Subject
D: Description
P: Position
S:NA   (for example) means that the factor S is nested in factors N and A (following Glass and Stanley, 1970). To test for this effect a quasi F test has been performed.

A comparison of the results for Noun-first condition in the two experiments shows that subjects in Experiment I recall considerably more adjectives than subjects in Experiment II (average 11·3 versus 8·7). That is, intentional recall is better than incidental recall. A comparison of results for Noun-end conditions, however, shows that recall in this case seems almost as high in Experiment II as in Experiment I (average 5·4 versus 5·7). *The specific instruction that the adjectives were to be recalled later on thus did not seem to have any facilitating influence in Noun-end conditions, and intentional and incidental recall turn out to be almost identical.*

Adjective order

Order of adjectives (A_1–A_5 versus A_5–A_1), moreover, is neither reflected as a significant main effect nor in significant interactions with other factors (Table 3).

Serial position of adjectives

So far, only total number of adjectives recalled is examined. Figures 5 and 6 show the positional recall of adjectives for Experiment I and Experiment II, respectively. (The corresponding tables are found in Appendix D, Tables D3 and D4.) Figures 5 and 6 might be a bit misleading. It must be remembered that different adjectives are tied to specific positions. The adjectives given in position 1 in Conditions I and III are given in position 5 in Conditions II and IV and vice versa. These specific adjectives, however, are never given in positions 2, 3 or 4. In the same way, the adjectives given in position 2 in Conditions I and III are given in position 4 in Conditions II and IV and vice versa. The adjectives given in position 3, on the other hand, were always given in that position.

This implies that the ease of remembering specific adjectives or adjective/noun combinations affects the form of the curves shown in Figs. 5 and 6. It should be remembered, however, that each curve represents the results for six different descriptions presented with two different orders of adjectives. Thus twelve different adjectives determine the points of the curve (except for the recall at position 3 where the same set of six adjectives enter twice). This variety of adjectives at each position counteracts the tendency for specific adjectives to determine the form of the curve. On the other hand, the adjectives in positions 1 and 5 tend to be the most strongly positive or the most strongly negative of the set of five. If such characteristics influence recall, the position of adjectives and degree of emotiveness may be confounded.

By comparing only position *1 and 5* and *2 and 4*, however, we compare the recall of *the same set of adjectives given in different positions*. Figure 7 shows these simplified curves for Experiment I, and Fig. 8 shows those for Experiment II.

Figures 7 and 8 indicate that the position of an adjective affects how well it will be retained, and that the effect of position is different in

Noun-first and Noun-end conditions. To test these effects of position as well as the effect of different descriptions, different analyses of variance have been performed. Separate analyses have been performed on the data from Experiment I and Experiment II.

Since different adjectives are tied to specific positions, only recall of adjectives in position 1 and position 5 are included in the analyses. Comparable analyses might also have been performed on the recall data of positions 2 and 4. In this case only t-tests have been used. The required analysis of variance is very complicated and does not yield sufficient additional information to be worth while.

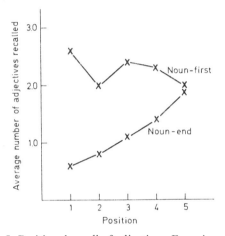

Fig. 5. Positional recall of adjectives. Experiment I.

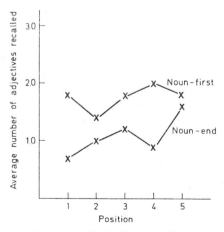

Fig. 6. Positional recall of adjectives. Experiment II.

In every experimental group 10 men and 10 women participated. When reporting the recall data, men and women are pooled together. A separate analysis for men and women, however, shows that the women recall more adjectives than the men. This holds for all four conditions in Experiment I and for every condition except one in Experiment II. Because of this, two separate analyses of variance, one

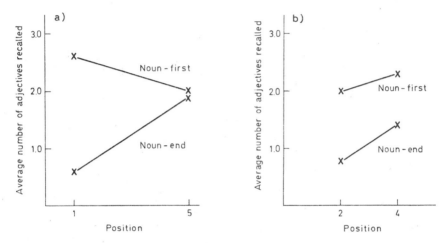

Fig. 7. Positional recall of adjectives. Positions 1 and 5 (a), and positions 2 and 4 (b). Experiment I.

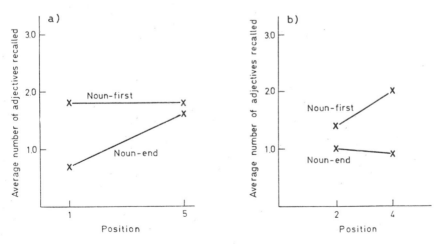

Fig. 8. Positional recall of adjectives. Positions 1 and 5 (a), and positions 2 and 4 (b). Experiment II.

for men and one for women, were performed on the data from Experiment I as well as for Experiment II, giving a total of four analyses of variance. Table 4 gives a summary of the significant effects found in these four analyses.

> These analyses of variance need some comments. When testing for significance, ordinary F tests have been used when possible. But for some of the effects no appropriate F ratio existed. In these cases a quasi F (F^1) ratio has been calculated following the procedure given in Winer (1962, p. 200–202). The degrees of freedom for the denominator have been determined following the suggestions there given.

> These complications stem from the decision that Description (D) in these experiments is best viewed as a random factor. Strictly following Glass and Stanley (1970, p. 473): "A factor may be considered random if the levels of that factor used in the study are a simple random sample from a population of levels with normally distributed effects." According to such criteria, the descriptions should not be considered a random factor because the descriptions used clearly are not a random sample of every description composed of five adjectives and a noun. On the other hand, as earlier explained, the descriptions are all carefully constructed.

> But, again following Glass and Stanley (*ibid.* p. 473): "Actually, the status (fixed or random) of a factor depends as much upon the population of replications of a study to which one wishes to generalize as it does upon the way in which levels were chosen." Such considerations make it reasonable to view Description as a random factor. We do not want to generalize the results found here only to further experiments using the identical descriptions. It seems more reasonable to generalize the result to a population of descriptions having the same general characteristics as those used in the experiments. If we were to continue explorations of coding strategies using descriptions of the form here used, we would not use identical descriptions over and over again.

The results for effect of Position are first of interest. No *main* effects of position are observed. When other experimental treatments are disregarded, position 1 is as good as position 5.

For Experiment I, however, Position and Noun show a significant interaction effect both for men and women. This means that the effect of moving an adjective from position 1 to position 5 is significantly different in Noun-first and Noun-end conditions. Substantially, this means simply that position 1 is optimal for recall in Noun-first conditions while position 5 is best in Noun-end conditions (Fig. 7). In Experiment II, no significant interaction between Position and Noun is displayed.

To test the effects of position further, t-tests for the difference between correlated pairs of means have been performed on the difference between recall in position 1 and position 5 in Noun-first and Noun-end conditions in Experiment I and Experiment II. Comparable analyses have also been performed on the recall data for position 2 versus position 4. In these analyses, the results for men and women have again been pooled together. Table 5 gives the results.

TABLE 5

Results of t-test used to test the differences in recall connected to position of adjectives.

Noun-position	Experiment	Positions	t	df.	p
Noun-first	I	1—5	1·97	39	
		2—4	1·08	39	
	II	1—5	0·19	39	
		2—4	1·99	39	≈0·05
Noun-end	I	1—5	5·78	39	0·001
		2—4	2·40	39	0·05
	II	1—5	3·68	39	0·001
		2—4	0·55	39	

The result of the t-tests show first that *the effect of position is much more prominent and more systematic in Noun-end than in Noun-first conditions.* In the former case, three out of four comparisons yield significance, while in the latter case one comparison gives results only approximating significance.

For Noun-end conditions, moreover, the results from Experiment I seem more consistent than the results from Experiment II. For Experiment I both of the possible comparisons give significant results. The effect of position seems to be rather systematic in this case (see Fig. 5). Although different adjectives are tied to different positions, the curve has a rather regular form. *The closer an adjective is to the noun, the better is the recall.*

When it comes to Experiment II, only the comparison between recall at positions 1 and 5 shows a significant difference. The results from positions 2 and 4 are in this case a little surprising. Although the difference is insignificant, the absolute difference is in the opposite direction of what would have been expected from the results of Experiment I. The adjectives at position 4 are less well retained than the adjectives at position 2 (Fig. 6). Except for the sudden drop at position 4, however, this curve is rather regular, as is the case for the comparable curve of Experiment I.

The analyses of variance summarized in Table 4 also provide information of effects of Noun position and Adjective sequence. The main effect of Noun is significant for three out of four analyses. The only exception is for men in Experiment II. However, the difference is in this case also in the expected direction.

Adjective sequence shows a main effect in one of the four analyses (Women, Experiment II). The women receiving the adjectives in the order A_1–A_5 show poorest recall. The women participating in the Noun-end condition in this case, however, seem to be an unusual group. This group of women is the only one out of eight to perform less well than the men in the recall task. It seems reasonable, therefore, that the unusual low performance of this specific group has lowered the total recall for the A_1–A_5 groups so substantially as to yield a significant main effect of adjective order.

Every one of the four analyses of variance summarized in Table 4 shows a highly significant effect of the interaction of Description, Position and Adjective order (DPA). The interaction between Position and Adjective order thus differs significantly over the six descriptions. When looking in detail at what an interaction between Position and

TABLE 6

An illustration of how specific adjectives are tied to Adjective order and Position for FARMER.

| | Position | |
	1	5
A_1—A_5	THICK (TETT)	FRIENDLY (VENNLIG)
A_5—A_1	FRIENDLY	THICK

Adjective order means in this special case, these results seem reasonable. The best way to do this is by way of the following table, Table 6, which shows how *specific adjectives* are tied to Position and Adjective order for one specific description; FARMER.

This table shows that the specific adjectives presented in position 1 when adjective order has been A_1–A_5, will be presented in position 5 when the order is A_5–A_1, and vice versa. This means that one specific adjective which is easy to remember in connection with the appropriate noun (for example, THICK to FARMER) gives a high score to position 1 in one case and to position 5 in another case.

The significant interaction between Description, Position and Adjective order is connected to this ease of recall of specific adjectives in connection with specific nouns, but means more specifically that *the relationship between the two adjectives with respect to ease of recall changes from description to description*. An example may be given from the results of men in Experiment I. In the description of FARMER there is a clear difference between the recall scores of THICK and FRIENDLY, the first adjective being recalled more frequently. For CHAIR, on the other hand, both of the adjectives in corresponding positions, SOFT and UGLY, are recalled almost equally well. Thus, the significant interaction turns out to be a trivial outcome of unintended, though "natural", differences between descriptions.

6.1.2. TOTAL NUMBER OF ADJECTIVES RETAINED VERSUS ADJECTIVES GIVEN BACK TO CORRECT NOUN

In addition to the adjectives given back in response to its appropriate noun, some of the adjectives used in the descriptions were given back to incorrect nouns. Figures 9 and 10 show curves for positional recall of all adjectives retained as well as curves for adjectives recalled to correct noun. (Total number of adjectives retained are found in Appendix D, in Tables D5 and D6.)

The difference between the two curves is much greater in Noun-end conditions than in Noun-first conditions. This is the case both for Experiment I and Experiment II. An analysis of variance performed on scores of difference between total number of adjectives retained and those given back to correct noun, shows a significant effect of noun position ($p < 0.001$, Table 7).

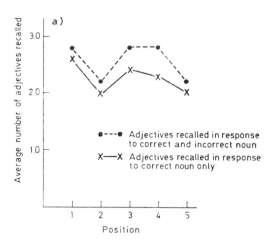

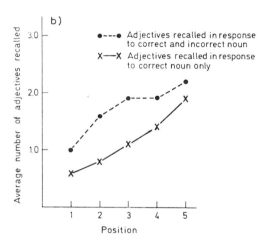

Fig. 9. Average number of adjectives recalled in response to correct and incorrect noun versus adjectives recalled in response to correct noun only. Noun-first conditions (a) and Noun-end conditions (b). Experiment I.

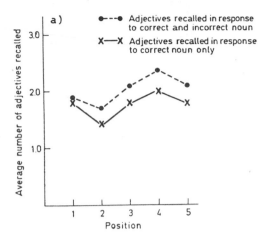

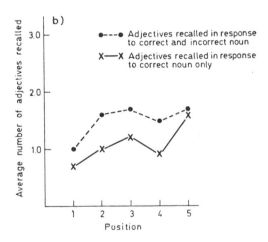

Fig. 10. Average number of adjectives recalled in response to correct and incorrect noun versus adjectives recalled in response to correct noun only. Noun-first conditions (a) and Noun-end conditions (b). Experiment II.

6.1.3. NOUN AS PROMPT WORD VERSUS FIRST ADJECTIVE AS PROMPT WORD
Recall of adjectives

Recall performance when the first adjective was used as the prompt word is shown in Figure 11. (The corresponding table is found in Appendix D, Table D7.) The results are compared to those observed when the noun function as a prompt for retrieval.

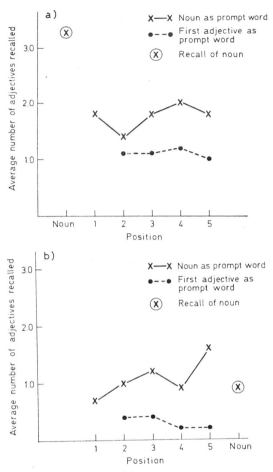

Fig. 11. Recall of adjective and nouns. Noun versus first adjective as prompt word. Noun-first conditions (a) and Noun-end conditions (b). Experiment II.

Figure 11 shows that the noun has been a superior prompt-word for the adjectives at every position both in Noun-first and Noun-end conditions. An analysis of variance (Table 8) shows that the effect of different prompt words is significant at the 0·001 level. The same analysis also shows a highly significant effect of Noun position (p < 0·001) as would have been expected from earlier analyses (Tables 3 and 4).

We see from Figure 11, moreover, that the effect of position is minimal when the first adjective functions as prompt word. The adjectives at positions 2, 3, 4 and 5 are recalled about equally well.

The analysis of variance reported in Table 8 is performed only on the data for recall of adjectives at positions 2, 3 and 4. When first adjective is used as prompt word, this means that one set of specific adjectives is used in A_1–A_5 conditions, another set in A_5–A_1 conditions. The set used as prompt words in A_1–A_5 conditions is included in the recall task for A_5–A_1 conditions and vice versa. Only the specific adjectives at positions 2, 3 and 4 are included in every recall task.

In the analysis of variance, a significant interaction between adjective sequence and kind of prompt word is revealed. The absolute difference between first adjective and noun as prompt words is different in A_1–A_5 and A_5–A_1 conditions. As different sets of adjectives serve as prompt words in these cases, these results are rather trivial. They only imply that the two sets of adjectives do not function equally well as prompt words for the remaining adjectives.

A significant interaction is also found between position of noun and adjective sequence. When going back to the data in this case, we notice that the absolute difference between recall in Noun-first and Noun-end conditions is much greater in A_1–A_5 conditions than in A_5–A_1 conditions. One of the reasons for this is that the subjects in Noun-end conditions in the former case performed rather poorly. One of the subgroups included is the special group of women mentioned before (p. 94), the only group of women to show poorer recall than the group of men. The unusual low score of these women may possibly have lowered the total score so substantially as to give the significant interaction.

TABLE 7

Analysis of variance of scores of difference between total number of adjectives recalled and those given back to correct noun.

Source	Sum of squares	df	Estimate	F	p
In	5·63	1	5·63	2·55	
N	50·63	1	50·63	22·94	0·001
A	0·90	1	0·90	0·41	
In × N	4·90	1	4·90	2·22	
In × A	0·63	1	0·63	0·28	
N × A	3·03	1	3·03	1·37	
In × N × A	0·40	1	0·40	0·18	
Within cells	335·50	152	2·21		

In: Instruction
N: Noun position
A: Adjective sequence

Recall of noun

Figure 11 also shows the average recall of nouns in Noun-first and Noun-end conditions, and we see that recall of nouns in Noun-first conditions is rather impressive. When adding nouns and adjectives recalled in this case, total recall actually approximates that for total recall with noun as prompt word (7·7 versus 8·7 words remembered on the average). The relationship between noun and first adjective is not symmetrical, however. When the noun is used as prompt word, the first adjective is correctly recalled on the average 1·8 times. When the first adjective is used as prompt word, the corresponding number for the noun is 3·3. In this special case, then, the "backward association" of the two is definitely the stronger one.

TABLE 8

Analysis of variance of recall of adjectives at positions 2, 3 and 4 using noun and first adjective as prompt word. Experiment II.

Source	Sum of squares	df	Estimate	F	p
Pr	146·31	1	146·31	53·96	0·001
N	195·81	1	195·81	72·21	0·001
A	0·31	1	0·31	0·11	
Pr × N	1·06	1	1·06	0·39	
Pr × A	13·81	1	13·81	5·09	0·05
N × A	15·01	1	15·01	5·53	0·05
Pr × N × A	5·26	1	5·26	1·94	
Within cells	412·15	152	2·71		

Pr: Prompt word
N: Noun position
A: Adjective sequence

In Noun-end conditions, on the other hand, recall of the noun cannot make up for the poor recall of the adjectives. When adding recall of adjectives and nouns in this case, 2·1 words are recalled on the average against an average of 5·4 adjectives when the noun has been prompt word.

The recall of the noun, however, is also in Noun-end conditions better than the recall of any one of the adjectives. The first adjective is a better prompt word for *the noun which appears at the end of the description than for its neighbouring adjective.* The total results from both Noun-first conditions and Noun-end conditions thus *demonstrates clearly that it is much easier to recall the noun than any of the adjectives.*

Retrieval of incorrect noun

The above results demonstrate clearly the unique function of the noun in retrieval of a description. This unique function is further illuminated by an additional analysis. When first adjective was used as prompt word, the subjects sometimes reproduced nouns from other descriptions. Among the adjectives also reproduced in these cases, some belong to the same description as *the noun incorrectly reproduced*, some to *the description to which the adjective prompt word belonged*. Table 9 shows the retrieval of adjectives in each of these categories, and it is seen that the number of adjectives connected to the incorrectly retrieved noun is much greater than the number of adjectives connected to the adjective prompt word. The difference is significant at the 0·001 level (t 5·50, df 48, t-test for correlated means).

TABLE 9

Retrieval of incorrect noun. Number of subjects showing this performance. Distribution of adjectives recalled in such cases. Total numbers.

Conditions		No. of subjects retrieving incorrect noun one or more times	Adjectives from the description of the incorrect noun	Adjectives from the description of the adjective prompt word
Noun-first	A_1–A_5	8	9	1
	A_5–A_1	13	35	4
Noun-end	A_1–A_5	14	20	3
	A_5–A_1	14	17	4
		49	81	12

6.2. Results from the impression formation tasks

In the impression formation data our primary interest concerns how adjective sequence affects how positive the entity described is judged to be: If the average rating is higher when the most positive adjectives are given in first positions than when given in last positions, a primacy effect is found. If the reverse is true a recency effect is found.

The reported results from the impression formation task in Experiment II are based on the 80 subjects who later on received the noun as prompt word in the recall task only. It might be argued that the results of all 160 subjects ought to be included since the impression formation task was identical whether the subsequent prompt word would be the noun or the first adjective. The decision to exclude half of the subjects, however, seems plausible for the following reasons:

The results from the remaining subgroup are, according to initial analyses, representative of the total group. When only this specific group is considered, furthermore, a comparison between recall and impression

formation data is possible. Both sets of data are then available from the
same subjects and from comparable groups in Experiment I and Experiment II. The present decision has also advantages of a more practical,
technical character. The analyses of variance to be performed on the
data from both of the experiments become much more complicated if
different numbers of subjects are included in the cells.

In the analysis, the categories of the rating scale were given numerical
values as follows: Extremely bad: 1, Very bad: 2, Bad: 3, Medium: 4,
Good: 5, Very good: 6, Extremely good: 7. The rating scale has furthermore been treated as an interval scale, assuming that the actual devia-
tion from the prerequisites for interval scaling would not be too great
and that the gains of treating it as an interval scale outweighs the loss in
exactness.

Table 10 shows the average difference per description in the direction
of primacy (P) or recency (R) for Noun-first and Noun-end conditions
in Experiments I and II. The results are presented separately for the
descriptions of CHAIR, ACTRESS and BOOK on the one hand, and
for SECRETARY, MOVIE and FARMER on the other. One of these
sets were given in approximately "descending order" of adjectives, the
other in approximately "ascending order" for any given group of subjects. Summing over all six descriptions, would therefore only cancel
out possible differences. The use of both "descending" and "ascending"
orders for each subject was motivated on the basis of our attempt to
control for "natural order" (p. 83).

Table II shows primacy effect (P) or recency effect (R) for each
description disregarding the magnitude of the effects. A minus is
inserted if reversal of order of adjectives is without any effect.

From the results in Tables 10 and 11 it appears that different order

TABLE 10

Average primacy and recency effects

| | Noun-first | | Noun-end | |
	CHAIR ACTRESS BOOK	SECRETARY MOVIE FARMER	CHAIR ACTRESS BOOK	SECRETARY MOVIE FARMER
Experi-ment I	P 0·02	P 0·62	R 0·73	R 0·48
Experi-ment II	P 0·22	R 0·17	R 0·20	R 0·35

TABLE 11

Primacy and recency effects in the impression formation data

Description	Experiment I		Experiment II	
	Noun-first	Noun-end	Noun-first	Noun-end
SECRETARY	P	R	P	P
CHAIR	R	R	P	P
MOVIE	P	R	R	R
ACTRESS	R	R	R	R
FARMER	P	—	—	R
BOOK	P	R	P	R

effects occurred in Noun-first and Noun-end conditions. From earlier experiments, *primacy effects* in Noun-first conditions were to be expected. Table 10 reveals two instances of primacy effects, one of recency effect and one instance with negligible order effect. An analysis of each description separately also reveals many exceptions to the rule of primacy, namely seven instances of primacy, four of recency and one showing no difference due to order.

In Noun-end conditions, on the other hand, more clear effects of order are observed. Averaging over three descriptions (Table 10) yields only *recency effects*. When each description is analysed separately (Table 11), nine cases of recency, two cases of primacy and one case of no difference are revealed.

TABLE 12

A summary of significant effects in two analyses of variance performed on the impression formation data

Source	Sum score of CHAIR, ACTRESS, BOOK	Sum score of SECRETARY, MOVIE FARMER
In		0·001
N		
A		
In × N		
In × A		
N × A	0·05	0·01
In × N × A		
Within cells		

In: Instruction
N: Noun position
A: Adjective sequence

Our tentative conclusion that different order effects hold for Noun-first and Noun-end conditions, is confirmed by two analyses of variance performed on the impression formation ratings. One analysis was performed on the sum score of CHAIR, ACTRESS and BOOK, and the other one on the sum score of SECRETARY, MOVIE and FARMER. Table 12 gives a summary of the significant effects in these two analyses.

The result of primary interest in this connection are the significant interactions between position of Noun (N) and sequence of adjectives (A) in both of the analyses. *The effect of reversing the order of the adjectives is thus significantly different in Noun-first and Noun-end conditions.*

The significant main effect of instruction in the analysis of the data from SECRETARY, MOVIE and FARMER is difficult to explain. The data show that the ratings in Experiment I are most favorable. But why should an instruction both *to remember and form impression* give higher ratings than an instruction only to form impressions? This seems particularly strange since it is the case for one set of descriptions only. For CHAIR, ACTRESS and BOOK the difference, though small, goes in the opposite direction.

To explore these effects of order still somewhat further, t-tests were performed on the differences due to adjective order. These t-tests were

TABLE 13

t-tests performed on differences due to adjective order

Noun position	Experiment	Descriptions	t	df	p
Noun-first	I	CHAIR, ACTRESS, BOOK	0·061	152	
		SECRETARY, MOVIE, FARMER	2·569	152	0·05
	II	CHAIR, ACTRESS, BOOK	0·741	152	
		SECRETARY, MOVIE, FARMER	0·694*	152	
Noun-end	I	CHAIR, ACTRESS, BOOK	2·719	152	0·01
		SECRETARY, MOVIE, FARMER	2·014	152	0·05
	II	CHAIR, ACTRESS, BOOK	0·741	152	
		SECRETARY, MOVIE, FARMER	1·458	152	

* In this case the difference has been in the opposite direction of what would have been expected. That is, it goes in the direction of recency.

performed on the sum score of CHAIR, ACTRESS and BOOK and also on the sum score of SECRETARY, MOVIE and FARMER. Table 13 shows the result of these tests.

Only three out of eight analyses give significant results. However, some vague pattern appears. *The results for Noun-end conditions are the most stable and show clearest effects of order of adjectives.* Every difference goes in the direction of recency, and two of them are statistically significant. Noun-first conditions, on the other hand, show only one significant primacy effect, and one of the observed differences also goes in the direction of recency.

The results of Experiment I reveals more effects of order of adjectives than is the case for Experiment II. Every significant effect is found in the former experiment. The differences in order effects between Experiment I and Experiment II is not significant when tested separately for each set of three descriptions in Noun-first and Noun-end conditions, however. (Test of interaction in four two-ways analyses of variance.) The overall trend of more order effect in Experiment I should not be ignored, however.

The general pattern in the impression formation data finally, is rather similar to that of the recall data (p. 93 and Table 5): Effects of position was found to be much more prominent in Noun-end than in Noun-first conditions, and, *within* the former conditions, also more consistent in Experiment I than in Experiment II.

7

Discussion of the Impression Formation Data

The weakest results in the present experiments were obtained in the impression formation part. Many subjects explicitly voiced their dissatisfaction with this task. Because the adjectives within some descriptions were experienced as conflicting, it was sometimes difficult to form impressions. Some subjects also reported that they felt that their checkmarks had been put down more or less at random. The impression formation data will for such reasons and also because less consistent data were obtained, be given less attention than the recall data. Nevertheless, however, the experiments provided some additional information to the impression formation tradition. One of the theoretically most interesting results is the significant interaction between position of noun and sequence of adjectives, showing *reversal of adjective order to have different consequences in Noun-first and Noun-end conditions*. A tendency towards primacy effects appears in Noun-first descriptions, whereas recency effects dominate in Noun-end descriptions.

In what follows we shall focus upon the impression formation data as such. A discussion of the relationship between impression formation and recall will be postponed until the recall data have been given closer consideration.

7.1. Order effects in the Louvain study

Before discussing order effects in the present experiments more thoroughly, a modified replication should be briefly discussed. This modified replication was conducted at the European Research Training Seminar in Experimental Social Psychology in Louvain in Belgium in 1967 (Jaspars *et al.* 1971).

The Louvain study differs from the present one in several ways: The descriptions were constructed according to different principles, and each description contained only four adjectives, as compared to five in the present study. The evaluative scores of the adjectives were known in advance, and the sequence of adjectives within a description was strictly ascending or descending.

The procedure was also modified in that the subjects in the Louvain study had to rate each impression on five scales. Three of these scales were evaluative scales and were later used in the analysis. The two additional scales served only as buffer scales. The subjects were given 30 seconds to rate their impression on all five scales. In contrast, only one scale was used in the present study, and the subjects had only four seconds to put down their check-marks. The Louvain study was similar to Experiment II in that no information about subsequent recall task was given in advance. Soldiers with rather low educational background were used as subjects.

In the Louvain study, *recency effects* were obtained both for Noun-first and Noun-end descriptions. The recency was stronger in the latter case, but the difference between Noun-first and Noun-end descriptions was not significant.

7.2. Order effects in Noun-first descriptions

Order effects in Noun-first descriptions will be discussed for Experiment I and Experiment II separately.

In Experiment II, a primacy effect was expected since the impression formation task in this case seems rather similar to other tasks giving such effects (p. 73). Contrary to the expectations, however, the results reveal only insignificant order effects, one in the direction of primacy, the other in the direction of recency (Table 10, p. 102, Table 13, p. 104).

We may ask, first of all, whether this unexpected result can be explained by the particular nature of our descriptions. Two factors will be considered in this connection: The difference between the first and last adjectives within a description with respect to evaluation, and a possible relationship between word openness and order effects.

As regards the first factor, it may be argued that the difference between first and last adjectives on an evaluative scale might have been too small to provide for clear order effects. This is not very likely to be the explanation, however. Three descriptions were given in a strict descending or ascending order. (SECRETARY, CHAIR, MOVIE, see Appendix C.) The average order effect for these particular descriptions was negligible (0·03). The difference in evaluative scores between first and last adjectives, however, was comparable in magnitude to those used in other studies in which clear primacy effect have been demonstrated (see, for example, Anderson and Barrios, 1961).

As for a possible relationship between word openness and order effects in impression formation, we shall offer no more than speculative comments. The latter will in part be based upon the explanation of primacy effects offered by Asch (1946), an explanation that clearly has had its opponents (e.g. Anderson and Hubert, 1963).

Asch tries to explain the primacy effect by suggesting that "the first terms set up in most subjects a *direction* which then exerts a continuous effect on latter terms" (*ibid.* p. 271). Asch's view thus seems to presuppose word openness.

In the present experimental set-up, the evaluative aspect of word meaning is of primary importance. To modify Asch's more general statement to fit this situation, it means that positive first words should influence subsequent words in such a way that their most positive potentialities would be selectively activated. Such an influence is possible, however, if and only if *subsequent words are relatively undetermined with respect to evaluation. And this is exactly what we tried to counteract in the construction of descriptions.* We tried to include two words which seemed to be positive independent of context in three descriptions and two words which seemed to be negative independent of context in the last three descriptions.

This explanation is only tentative and difficult to test against available data because most often sufficient details are not reported. It is interesting to note, however, that the most positive words in Asch's experiment VI, INTELLIGENT, INDUSTRIOUS, do not seem to be as unequivocally positive as for example, BEAUTIFUL, PLEASANT.

If the suggested explanation has something to offer, it testifies to the need for great care when order effects are to be predicted. Extreme care seems also warranted on the basis of the considerable number of factors which have been shown to influence order effects (Jaspars *et al.* 1971). The impression formation task as such seems to provide for use of different strategies, and order effects are in turn rather susceptible to such variations in strategies.

One possible factor affecting strategy should be mentioned in this connection. This factor has been given too little attention, and seems to impose restrictions on generalization from the present as well as from many other previous studies. What we have in mind, is how strategy and hence nature of order effects may vary from one category of subjects to another.

Consider, for instance, the recency effect in the Louvain study (Jaspars *et al.* 1971) and the fact that soldiers with rather low educational background were used as subjects in that case. In the studies by Asch (1946), by Anderson and Barrios (1961), by Anderson and Hubert (1963), and by McGinnis and Oziel (1970) as well as in the present study, students have been subjects. In the study by Luchins (1966a) the subjects were at the high school and at the college level. It may hence be argued that recency effect may be due to strategies adopted by subjects with lower intellectual-educational status.

The studies by Mayo and Crockett (1964) and by Margulis, Costanzo and Klein (1971) lend some support to this explanation. In the latter study boy scouts (11–16 years old) attending a summer camp were the subjects. In a task similar to the traditional impression formation, *recency* effects were again obtained.

The results from the Mayo and Crockett study indicate, more generally, that different categories of subjects may process information in different ways. In their study subjects were presented with two blocks of opposite information about a person. They found that *cognitively simple subjects* (as determined by Kelly's Role Construct Repertory Test) showed a much greater recency effect in forming an impression about a person than *cognitively complex persons*. The latter ended up with almost truly ambivalent impressions.

There are, however, considerable differences between the Mayo and Crockett study and the Louvain study. For one thing, Mayo and Crockett's subjects were asked to report their impressions after each block of opposite information, and this procedure has been shown to give results different from those obtained when impressions are reported at the end of the description only (Luchins, 1958). The studies are thus not strictly comparable. The essential point is, however, that Mayo and Crockett have demonstrated *that different types of subjects may process opposing information in different ways.*

It seems to be a reasonable supposition that students as a group will be cognitively more complex than soldiers with low educational background. Different strategies giving results indicative of different order effects may hence be expected on the basis of the results of Mayo and Crockett.

More generally, this implies some uncertainty as to possible generalization of the present impression formation results to other categories of subjects. The same uncertainty also pertains to generalizations from other studies within this area.

In Experiment I, the set consisting of SECRETARY, MOVIE and FARMER reveals a significant primacy effect. It seems questionable, however, if this result should be given any weight. Although the primacy effect as such is statistically significant in this case, the order effect of Experiment I is *not* significantly different from the order effect in Experiment II (p. 105). In our earlier notes on expectations concerning order effects, we referred to the study by Anderson and Hubert (1963). We notice that the results of the present study with *postponed recall* came out differently from what was the case in their study in which more immediate recall was required. In the latter study, a weak recency effect was obtained.

7.3. Order effects in Noun-end descriptions

The noun at the end of the descriptive adjectives represents a novel variation of impression formation designs, and the results are for that reason of particular interest. In the case where only impression formation was initially asked for, that is, in Experiment II, recency effects were found, but these effects were not significant. (Table 10, p. 102, Table 13, p. 104).

In the Louvain study (Jaspars *et al.* 1971) a recency effect was also found for Noun-end descriptions. This result seems at first to support the results of the present experiment. Uncertainty exists, however, as to how to interpret the results from the Louvain study. The soldiers used as subjects in this case, show recency effects both for Noun-first and Noun-end descriptions. The recency effect was stronger in the latter case, but not significantly stronger. It is difficult to know if the recency effect for Noun-end descriptions depends on the position of the noun or on more general characteristics of the coding strategies used by this category of ιbjects. It could therefore be questioned to what extent it is possible to generalize the results here obtained.

When turning to the results of Experiment I, it will be noted that stronger and significant recency effects were obtained in this case (Table 10, p. 102, Table 13, p. 104). When these effects are tested against the order effects found in Experiment II, the differences are not significant (p. 105).

At present then, it seems reasonable to conclude that some uncertainty still exists as to order effects in impression formation in cases where the entity to be described is mentioned after the adjectives describing it. Although more experimentation is needed at this point, however, the results at hand suggest rather strongly that such effects will go in the direction of recency. In every case known, the observed effects have this direction. *The significant difference* in order effects between Noun-first and Noun-end descriptions in the present study is also of importance in this connection. It is furthermore reasonable to keep in mind that the descriptions used probably have characteristics that might work against order effects.

The results thus seem mostly in accordance with the expectation of recency. If recency effects should repeatedly be found with noun at the end, it must be questioned more closely how this effect is to be explained. In the decoding strategies depicted in Fig. 1, p. 58, it seems to be suggested that every adjective is present when the noun is given. At this point the possibility both for "backwards" and "forwards" processing of adjectives should logically be present. That is, logically, it should be possible to "go" back to the first adjective presented and start further processing from this point, or it should be possible to start processing with the adjective closest to the noun. A recency effect suggests "backwards" processing, either because the last-mentioned adjectives are in a way more salient or because they direct the processing of the other words in accordance with Asch's explanation of order effects. When the memory results are discussed some further comments on this point will be given (pp. 142–143).

8

Discussion of the Recall Data

In this discussion, the very clear difference in recall between Noun-first and Noun-end descriptions will be in focus. The discussion has two related aims. The first aim is to explore the *generality* of the results obtained. A number of other studies investigating effects of noun position will be reported, and some possible limitations to the superiority of Noun-first will be discussed. This observed superiority may possibly be related *to the openness of the adjectives* and to *how concrete the nouns are*. Concreteness of nouns, moreover, borders on the general issue of word openness.

The second aim is to try to explain the clear difference in recall in a way consistent with the more detailed results from the experiments. Two main approaches will be explored. An attempt will be made to relate *models of decoding strategies* to *memory processes*, since the observed differences in recall may be related to differences in memory processes. The Noun-first and Noun-end descriptions may also provide for different opportunities for *integration of the description*, and this possibility will also be explored.

8.1. The superiority of Noun-first

The results from the recall tasks show very convincingly that more adjectives are remembered when the noun is given *ahead of* as compared to *at the end of* the description (Figs. 3 and 4, p. 86), and this is the case whether the noun or the first adjective is used as prompt word (Table 8, p. 100). This result, furthermore, is very consistent and is replicated across a set of different variations. The subjects may thus be warned of the recall task as in Experiment I, or the recall task may come without prior warning as in Experiment II. The difference in recall due to noun position comes out clearly in both cases. The superiority of recall in Noun-first conditions also holds when each description is analysed separately although they differ significantly with respect to ease of recall.

The superiority of Noun-first cannot be explained by reference to the use of *the first word* versus *the last word* as prompt word, but is clearly also related to the specific *function* of the word within the description. A comparison between the two different conditions in which the first word has been used as prompt word strongly supports this conclusion. In one case the first word was an adjective, and the average number of words recalled was 2·1. In the case where the first word was a noun, the average number of words recalled was 8·7, i.e. more than four times as great (Appendix D, Tables D2 and D7).

The observed very strong effects of noun position in this study are also supported by evidence from other experiments. First to be mentioned is the modified replication of parts of the present study—the so-called Louvain study (Jaspars *et al.* 1971)—already discussed in connection with the impression formation data (p. 106). This study also included an incidental recall task where the nouns of the descriptions were used as prompt words. Over-all recall was much poorer in the Louvain study than in the present one. This may at least in part be explained by the more complicated and time-using procedure used to rate impressions and also by the different categories of subjects in the two experiments. *In spite of these variations, however, the effect of position of noun within a description was very much the same.* About twice as many adjectives were recalled in Noun-first as in Noun-end conditions in the Louvain study.

The importance of the position of noun has also been corroborated in experiments on recall with no request for impression formation. A short-term memory variation of the present study has been performed by the American student Alice Katagari (1969) as part of her course work. Her material was ten descriptions composed of five adjectives and a noun where the noun was presented either ahead of, or at the end of the series of five adjectives. Every subject, ten in all, received descriptions of both forms.

In the experiment, one particular description was first presented to the subjects. Immediately afterwards they were given a number, their task being to write down numbers counting backwards by threes. After a period of this intervening activity (unfortunately Katagari does no report for how long it lasted), the subjects were stopped, given the noun and asked to write down the adjectives connected to it. The adjectives from the descriptions with noun first were recalled significantly better than adjectives from descriptions with the noun at the end also in this short-term-memory task.

Languages differ with respect to sequence of adjectives and nouns in phrases consisting of one noun, and one or more adjectives. In Norwegian, the adjectives come ahead of the noun (unless a relative clause is used to secure pre-position of the noun as in this study). In French, however, the noun is often followed by the adjectives.

On the basis of the superiority of recall observed for descriptions with noun first, it might be expected that Frenchmen recalling French phrases would perform better than Norwegians recalling the corresponding Norwegian phrases. Such expectations were tested out by Skjerve (1971).

He constructed a set of 17 different phrases with equivalents both in French and Norwegian. Examples of the phrases are:

EN AFRIKANSK ELEFANT—UN ELEPHANT AFRICAN (An African elephant)

EN USTABIL OG MOTSTRIDENDE OPINION—UNE OPINION INSTABLE ET CONTRADICTOIRE (An unstable and contradictory opinion).

The set of 17 phrases was read aloud as one continuous text. The subjects were asked to remember the words and write them down after having listened to the whole set. The answer sheets contained fragments of every phrase, leaving an open space for the adjectives which the subjects had to fill in.

Nine Norwegian students, and nine French students served as subjects and the French and the Norwegian group performed equally well on a pretest for recall consisting of 15 unconnected adjectives.

The results from the experiment on phrases, however, showed that the French students recalled significantly more adjectives than the Norwegian students. Phrases with noun first thus again showed their superiority regarding recall of adjectives. Such results are also consistent with the findings in the learning experiment by Lambert and Paivio (1956) discussed earlier (pp. 69–70).

Thus, the superiority of recall of adjectives in the sequence *noun-adjective* as compared to *adjective-noun* has been confirmed in a variety of different situations. In Experiment II in this study, as well as in the Louvain study (Jaspars *et al.* 1971) incidental recall was tested, in Experiment I the subjects were given the double instruction of both recall and impression formation, while in the studies by Katagari (1969), Skjerve (1971) and Lambert and Paivio (1956) only recall was asked for. The same effect of noun position is, furthermore, observed whether the material to be remembered is presented only once or several times.

Two more observations are also of interest in this connection. Teleman *et al.* (1973, pp. 60–61) report that a text becomes more difficult to read if it contains a great number of determining words, as, e.g. adjectives, in prenominal position.

The sign language of the deaf provides the second observation. In the discussion of a set of experiments performed to explore syntactic aspects of the Israeli sign language, Schlesinger (1972) reports that *in signing the noun always was given ahead of its modifying adjective.* In the Hebrew language, the same order is also found, however. But Schlesinger suggests that this order may be found in sign language irrespective of the sequence of noun-adjective in the national oral language. As support it is noted that the noun-adjective order also is found in the sign language used in Germany, whereas the opposite is true of the oral language in this case.

8.2. Word openness and the superiority of Noun-first

The superiority of Noun-first over Noun-end appears at this point to be firmly documented. The study by Rommetveit and Turner (1967), however, gave results that from one point of view might be interpreted as contradictory. In order to explore some necessary conditions for the superiority of Noun-first, it seems therefore reasonable briefly to return to this study. One specific difference between this study and the present, that is, the difference between *open adjectives* and *adjectives carefully defined* (see p. 71) should be discussed in relation to the other studies using the Noun-first, Noun-end variation. Is it possible to maintain that the superiority of Noun-first depends on open adjectives when these studies also are taken into consideration?

The studies of most interest in this connection is the one by Lambert and Paivio (1956) and the one by Katagiri (1969). In addition, some specific results from the present experiments seem revealing.

The study by Lambert and Paivio seems the most intriguing one. Their experimental set-up was a learning situation where the material to be learned was presented *several times*. It might hence be suggested that the adjectives were open only *on the first presentation*. On the second presentation it would already be known to which noun they were connected, and their more specific meaning would thus by then be available. If this were so, the difference between Noun-first and Noun-end should either be wholly explained by *differences on the first trial* or word openness should not be so decisive as suggested above.

However, the subjects were presented with a list of 28 words, and nothing was said about its internal structure. In addition, the anticipation method used seems to emphasize connections between adjacent words rather than—at least for most adjectives—the more remote noun. Most probably, such factors work against a rapid formation of connections between adjectives and noun. The Lambert and Paivio study can thus hardly be interpreted as providing unequivocal evidence against the hypothesis that Noun-first superiority is contingent upon relatively open adjectives.

The study by Katagiri may possibly be used to explore this relationship somewhat further. The subjects in her study knew from the instruction that only different kinds of persons would be described. This information should thus eliminate some of the meaning potentialities of the adjectives, even though not to the degree of specification obtained in the Rommetveit and Turner study. In order to illustrate this, the set of adjectives used to describe SECRETARY in the present experiments, SEVERE, COOL, EXTRAORDINARY, BEAUTIFUL, PLEASANT, may be reconsidered. If it were known that some kind of person was being described, meaning potentialities of relevance to, for example, WINTER and CLIMATE would certainly be irrelevant. Determination of meaning appears to be a relative affair, however, ranging from almost total openness to nearly complete referential specification. Thus, different potentialities will still be activated by the adjectives listed above, depending upon whether they refer to A SECRETARY or A LOVER or A MAN.

The descriptions of the present study were constructed in such a way as to ensure considerable openness. The effect of noun position in the study by Katagiri indicates that this effect is not dependent on carefully constructed word combinations, and such a conclusion is also warranted in view of some additional observations from the present experiments. The redundancy task (Appendix A) showed that the sets of adjectives describing persons were more suggestive of the "correct" noun than was the case for the sets of adjectives describing things or happenings. This difference, however, did not influence the effect of the position of the noun. The ratio between recall of adjectives in Noun-first versus Noun-end conditions was almost identical for these two sets of nouns. But although carefully constructed combinations of adjectives are not required, it is still reasonable to conclude that the results from the relevant studies have not contradicted the hypothesis that Noun-first superiority depends on relatively open adjectives.

Another characteristic of descriptions that seems to deserve closer attention is the extent to which they initiate or invite the formation of visual images. Rommetveit and Turner refer to this characteristic when discussing differences obtained between descriptions *within* their study. In addition to descriptions of the form A LEFTWARD, JAGGEDLY DESCENDING, BROKEN CURVE versus A JAGGED, BROKEN CURVE DESCENDING LEFTWARD descriptions like A SMALL, FILLED AND TILTED SQUARE versus A SQUARE, SMALL, FILLED AND TILTED were also used. For the latter descriptions, almost identical recall was reported for the two versions.

In the discussion of why no difference was observed in this case, Rommetveit and Turner suggest different possible factors. A most interesting possibility is that the difference in results between CURVE and SQUARE might be related to the ease of *visual image formation*.

When finishing their recall tasks, the subjects were asked whether they had formed visual images when listening to the descriptions. This turned out to be the case very frequently for descriptions like SQUARE, but was extremely seldom reported for descriptions like CURVE. *It is also reported that visualization was facilitated when the noun was given ahead of the adjectives:* To form visual images of "filledness" and "tiltedness" was more easy when it was known that these were characteristics of SQUARE. The facilitation of formation of visual images when the noun comes first, may thus be a factor of importance.

Inherent in such a conclusion is the presupposition that visual images have functional importance in tasks of memory. This seems rather well documented by Paivio (1969). Paivio also maintains that visual images are related to the abstractness/concreteness of the words in such a way that they are aroused most frequently in response to the concrete words. In special experiments (Paivio, 1963) words of general reference/specific reference were used to exemplify the dimension abstract/concrete (ex. PERSON—MAN). It may be argued that an analogous difference holds between CURVE and SQUARE. The difference with respect to frequence of imagery between CURVE and SQUARE, then, is in good correspondence with the view of Paivio.

Sequence effects may thus possibly be contingent upon abstractness/concreteness of the nouns. In the studies referred to earlier, as well as in the present study, mostly concrete nouns have been used. The studies by Skjerve (1971) and Lambert and Paivio (1956) include some more abstract nouns, although the majority of nouns in these studies also were concrete. In reports of recall data, however, the results of descriptions are pooled. It is therefore impossible to reanalyze their results and explore whether order effects vary with the abstractness/concreteness of the nouns.

The only exception to the general superiority of Noun-first in the present experiments, was interestingly for MOVIE in Experiment II. In this case Noun-end conditions gave slightly better recall. MOVIE seems, subjectively, to be the less concrete among the set of nouns ACTRESS, MOVIE, FARMER, CHAIR, BOOK, SECRETARY.

Little is at present known about the issue of concreteness/abstractness and order effects. The concreteness/abstractness of adjectives as well as nouns may be of importance (Yuille, Paivio and Lambert, 1969). A reasonable implication of the discussion above, however, seems to be a reservation concerning the empirically firmly established superiority of Noun-first against Noun-end: *This superiority has so far only been clearly documented for rather concrete nouns.*

We may also speculate whether—and if so, how—abstractness/concreteness of nouns is related to word openness. It may be argued that abstract nouns generally are more open and more context-dependent than concrete nouns. If this is so, postponement of decoding should be expected when an abstract noun appears first in a description. Subsequent adjectives would then actually serve the purpose of further specification, and the differences between decoding strategies in Noun-first and Noun-end conditions would level out. Such speculations direct our attention towards the oversimplified character of descriptions of decoding strategies offered so far. These descriptions may give the impression that decoding is *either* cumulative or postponed, and that the two possibilities are opposite and conflicting. Strategies may be composed of both cumulative and postponed decoding, however, and modification may proceed from noun to adjective and vice versa.

8.3. Decoding strategies and memory processes

In what follows, we shall try to explore some possible relationships between decoding strategies and memory processes. The reason is simply that such relationships may partly explain the striking difference in recall of adjectives between Noun-first and Noun-end descriptions. By pursuing this issue, moreover, we shall try to relate rather closely the results from two different areas, the psychology of language and the psychology of memory, two areas between which too little contact has been established (Fillenbaum, 1971, 1973).

As a consequence of such a theoretical analysis some specific problems became of importance. Two small experiments were performed to explore these problems empirically, and those experiments will also be reported in this part.

There are different conceptions of memory, and no attempt will be made here to weigh them against each other. The most widely held view at present is that memory is composed of three different stores, sensory store, short-term store (STS) and long-term store (LTS) (see for example Atkinson and Shiffrin, 1968).[1] In the present discussion a somewhat different conceptual framework, that by Craik and Lockhart, will serve as our point of departure (Craik and Lockhart, 1972, Craik, 1973). This latter alternative has been preferred because its core concepts are more in agreement with the conceptual framework already introduced.

8.3.1. THE CONCEPTUAL FRAMEWORK OF CRAIK AND LOCKHART

Craik and Lockhart (Craik and Lockhart, 1972; Craik, 1973) have suggested, as an alternative to multistore theories of memory, that human memory may be described in terms of *depths or levels of processing*.

A main point in their conceptual framework is a rather direct linking

1. It should be noticed that short-term *store* and long-term *store* is used by Atkinson and Shiffrin when referring to the two hypothetical storage systems. Short-term memory and long-term memory is used operationally, referring to experimental situations requiring material to be stored over short or long time respectively. We shall use the terms in a similar way.

of *memory traces* to *perceptual analyses*. According to many theorists (e.g. Sutherland, 1968), perception involves the rapid analysis of stimuli. Early stages concerns the analysis of more directly physical or sensory characteristics such as lines, angles, pitch, etc. Later stages concern pattern recognition and finally also meaning and meaning elaboration. In connection with such descriptions of perceptual analysis, the expression "depth of processing" is often used. The "deeper" the analysis, the more semantic and cognitive factors become involved.

As mentioned, perceptual analysis and memory traces are rather closely linked together, and Craik and Lockhart make the specific suggestion that the persistence of a memory trace is related to the depth of perceptual analysis. In their own words (Craik and Lockhart, 1972, p. 675):

> One of the results of this perceptual analysis is the memory trace. Such features of the trace as its coding characteristics and its persistence thus arise essentially as byproducts of perceptual processing.[1] Specifically, we suggest that trace persistence is a function of depth of analysis, with deeper levels of analysis associated with more elaborate, longer lasting, and stronger traces. Since the organism is normally concerned only with the extraction of meaning from the stimuli, it is advantageous to store the products of such deep analyses, but there is usually no need to store the products of preliminary analyses.

If only products of deep analyses are stored, this certainly has implications for the problem of re-encoding. When verbatim recall is observed some time after presentation, is this to be understood as *recall of word form as such* or as *re-encoding of meaning into exactly the same form*? We shall return to such problems later on (p. 143).

The concept of *level* or *stage* of perceptual analysis presented above, does not imply discontinuity. According to Craik and Lockhart, perceptual analysis should be viewed as essentially continous. Accordingly, the persistence of memory also varies along a continuum from the very transient memory of sensory analyses to long lasting memories of semantic elaborations.

The general scheme outlined above, must not be interpreted too literally. Some modifications seem possible, and processing does not always proceed through a fixed sequence of necessary levels. The open attitude towards possible modifications, however, does not seem to solve

---

1. Craik and Lockhart refer in this connection to Morton, 1970.

one problem inherent in the general outline. The emphasis on perceptual analyses as essentially continous tends to ignore or camouflage the problem of the *qualitative change between semantic and non-semantic processing*. Problems pertaining to qualitative change have not been discussed.

In addition to the memory system outlined, Craik and Lockhart also suggest a second way in which stimuli can be retained. *It is also possible to recirculate information at a given level of processing.* Such a recirculation is possible at different levels of processing. Most probably, however, information at different levels differs with respect to the ease of recirculation. It seems to be the case that the results of early sensory analyses are particularly difficult—probably impossible—to recirculate, while the results of other analyses, as for example phonemic[1] analyses, are easy to recirculate.

A prerequisite for recirculation is that the information to be recirculated is attended to. As soon as attention is diverted, the process of forgetting will start. The forgetting rate as such depends on the depth to which the material had been processed prior to the period of recirculation: The deeper the material has been processed, the slower becomes the rate of forgetting.

The framework of Craik and Lockhart is very open towards the use of different strategies in different situations. How a specific material will be processed, to which level, and to what extent recirculation will be involved, depends on the kind of material being processed and also on the specific demands imposed on the subjects. A rather similar position is also adopted by Helstrup (1973).

Some limitations, however, are inherent in the system in the form of *capacity limitations*. According to usual conceptions of memory in terms of three different memory stores, one characteristic associated with short-term store is its relatively small capacity. The concept of limited capacity may be understood in somewhat different ways. It may be taken to be limitation in storage capacity, in processing capacity, or in some interaction between these possibilities. Craik and Lockhart (1972) state explicitly that the term capacity in their conceptual framework refers to *limitations on processing*. The limitation with respect to storage is conceived of as a direct consequence of this more basal limitation.

The processing capacity available, then, may be used in different

---

1. It has been discussed whether such analyses are acoustic or articulatory. In order to avoid this discussion, the form "phonemic" is used in this presentation as suggested by Schulman (1971).

ways. It may be used to process some material to deeper levels or it may be used to recirculate the material at a given, specific level. In the latter case, the amount of material which can be handled depends on the level at which this recirculation takes place. At deeper levels, the individual may use prior knowledge to a greater extent and thus handle the material more efficiently.

Different sets of data may serve as empirical anchoring of the conceptual framework of Craik and Lockhart. Of special interest in the following discussion are the data from studies on incidental learning. Craik and Lockhart (1972) relate results from particular experiments to their conceptions. Only the general expectations concerning incidental learning will be referred to here, however. If memory traces are directly related to levels of processing, different kinds of relationships should pertain to incidental and intentional learning. This suggestion is in correspondence with the position of Postman (1968) in his review of incidental learning (see pp. 68–69). The assumed relationship between levels of processing and memory traces allows for the following more specific expectations concerning intentional and incidental learing:

(a) If the stimulus material is processed to deeper levels in the intentional task than in the incidental learning task, superior recall performance is to be expected in the former.
(b) If the stimulus material is processed to similar levels in the incidental and intentional learning tasks, similar recall performance should also be expected.
(c) If the strategy spontaneously adopted by subjects in a specific learning task involves processing to less deep levels than required for a given incidental learning task, superior recall performance should be found for incidental learning.

As already mentioned, the system proposed by Craik and Lockhart with its emphasis on concepts like processing and strategies, seems at first glance to be very much in line with the general framework outlined in preceeding parts of this monograph. Consider, for instance, our conception of word meaning as a process initiated by an act of reference followed by representational, associative and emotive components (p. 40). Such a model of meaning is in some respect isomorphic to the model of perceptual analysis as a continuous process proceeding from an initial concentration on sensory dimensions to later stages of semantic elaborations. The latter model, however, must also cope with the problem of the transition from non-semantic to semantic processing.

The similarity between Craik and Lockhart's model of levels of processing and our approach to word meaning stands out even more clearly when we consider traditional models of memory and how meaning or semantic coding enters the discussion of memory stores. A controversial point in this connection has been whether semantic coding is possible in short-term store, or if such coding is confined to long-term store (see Schulman, 1971, 1972). The discussion of semantic coding then becomes a question of *semantic coding* versus *no semantic coding at all*, and such a dichotomy appears to mirror a rather static conception of meaning.

The conceptual framework of Craik and Lockhart raises some specific problems, however. Several of the experiments on memory which will be referred to are written within the store tradition. In our discussion of data from such experiments, we have to make post facto estimates concerning the level to which the material has been processed.

It has often been maintained that phonemic coding is all that is found in STS and that semantic coding is confined to LTS (Baddeley and Dale, 1966; Kintsch and Busche, 1969). Schulman (1971) argues against such a view and maintains that the experiments in support of it are such that phonemic coding is the only possibility available or the only efficient strategy in that particular experimental set-up. In the other kinds of experiments, semantic coding is demonstrated for STS as well (Schulman, 1972). In the traditional STS experiments digits or letters are often used as stimulus material, and in cases where verbal material is employed, no requirements for semantic coding are included. Time limits for processing are in addition usually rather narrow. It seems reasonable, therefore, that coding under such conditions takes place at a pre-semantic level.

Although we shall follow Craik and Lockhart, many of the implications for interpretation of the recall data in the present experiment would also follow from the store conception of Atkinson and Shiffrin (1968) according to which semantic coding is confined to LTS. Convergence at this level shows that these different views of memory after all have much in common, and a point made by Helstrup (1973, p. 31) helps to clarify this similarity. In the terminology of Atkinson and Shiffrin, verbal material is stored in an auditive-verbal-linguistic form in STS, and they suggest that this kind of storing is a consequence of structural characteristics of STS. It is, however, possible to consider the auditive-verbal-linguistic component as a control-operation, as something which is done to the information or to the material. If so, the

auditive-verbal-linguistic component becomes rather similar to processing to pre-semantic levels.

8.3.2. "LEVELS OF PROCESSING" AND THE PRESENT RESULTS

How does the conceptual framework of Craik and Lockhart bear upon
our preliminary models of decoding strategies and the results obtained
in our recall tests? In what follows, an attempt will be made to reformu-
late our preliminary models of decoding strategies in correspondence
with the terminology offered by Craik and Lockhart. We shall examine,
furthermore, if the recall results from the present study are compatible
with such a reformulation:
(a) Does the difference in *total-recall* between Noun-first and Noun-end
    descriptions fit?
(b) Is *the differential effect of instruction* between Noun-first and Noun-end
    conditions explainable?
(c) Are the *serial position curves* obtained compatible with predictions
    based upon such a conceptual framework?

Craik and Lockhart's memory model relates to the descriptions of
decoding strategies in Noun-first and Noun-end conditions in the
following way: When the noun is given ahead of the adjectives, we
argued that the adjectives can be fully decoded immediately and modify
the impression of what is already presented in a cumulative way. In the
terminology of Craik and Lockhart this means that *processing can proceed
to rather deep levels rather quickly*. The memory traces thus immediately
become rather persistent. When the noun is given at the end of the
series of adjectives, however, the adjectives remain relatively undetermined until the noun is presented. This implies that the adjectives at
first are processed to some rather "shallow" level only and are recirculated at this level until the noun is given.

An interesting question pertains to the *quality* of this "shallow" processing. The latter may be conceived of as processing to pre-semantic
levels only or to "initial" semantic levels in accordance with what has
earlier been said about the autonomy of words (see p. 53). In the subsequent discussion, the most extreme view will first be adopted, i.e. we
shall assume that processing of adjectives is only phonemic until the
noun is given. Towards the end of the discussion of memory processes
and decoding strategies, we shall be in a better position to evaluate the
two possibilities.

If we assume "shallow" pre-semantic processing, we must expect five adjectives to be recirculated at a phonemic level. The question is then whether the capacity for processing is great enough to recirculate every one of the five adjectives. It is not easy to estimate how many elements can be recirculated at a specific level. From studies of memory span (Miller, 1956) we would expect that five adjectives should fall within such limits. In the studies on which Miller has based his estimate, however, the material may very well be processed far beyond what is the case for adjectives in our Noun-end conditions.[1] More recent estimates of the short-term component are therefore probably of more direct relevance. Baddeley (1970) estimates the short-term component in free recall to be 2–3 items.

It is thus rather uncertain whether every one of the five adjectives can be recirculated. If not, some adjectives may possibly be lost already at the moment when the noun is presented. The answer to this question depends on the rate of forgetting at a phonemic level of analysis, and an experiment by Peterson and Peterson (1959) seems to be of relevance in this connection. They found that subjects very seldom would remember a 3-consonant syllable (for example, CHJ) after 18 seconds if they were required to count backwards in steps of three during this period to prevent rehearsal. The longer the subjects had to store the 3-consonant syllable, the greater the chance that it was lost, and a marked loss was found after only 3 seconds. In the present experiment it takes from 7·5 to 10 seconds to present the five adjectives within a description. According to the data of Peterson and Peterson some adjectives may thus very well be lost before the noun is presented.

A reformulation of decoding strategies in accordance with Craik and Lockhart's memory model thus seems to fit the main results as far as *total recall* is concerned. In Noun-first conditions the description may immediately be processed to rather deep levels corresponding to rather persistent memory traces. In Noun-end condition, on the other hand, this depth of processing cannot be achieved until the noun is given. Because of the rapid forgetting rate of items processed to prior levels, some adjectives are already lost, and *only some part of the description* may be processed to those deeper levels providing for more persistent memory traces.

---

1. This point is somewhat further elaborated in a discussion of the learning of lists of unconnected items on pp. 132–133.

The differential effect of instruction between Noun-first and Noun-end conditions also becomes understandable within such a frame. For Noun-first conditions, the warned recall in Experiment I was higher than the unwarned recall in Experiment II. For Noun-end conditions, on the other hand, total recall was rather similar in both experiments (pp. 88–89). According to our discussion of incidental recall, superior recall is to be expected for intentional recall when such tasks allow processing to keeper levels (p.122). When comparing Noun-first descriptions in Experiment I and Experiment II, processing to deeper levels may very well have been performed in the former case. In both experiments, the descriptions must be processed to a semantic level because of the impression formation task. A request for an evaluation of the entity described only—as in Experiment II—may only require processing to relatively "superficial" semantic levels, however. In Experiment I in which a recall task was expected as well, processing to more elaborate semantic levels may very well form part of the subject's strategy to facilitate recall. They would then attempt to *integrate* all components of the descriptions as firmly as possible, and such integration presuppose more elaborate processing. (For further comments to this point, see p. 149.)

In Noun-end conditions, on the other hand, the processing capacity should be used exclusively to recirculate as many adjectives as possible at a phonemic level until the noun is presented. This effort to recirculate should be identical in Experiment I and Experiment II because it is a requirement inherent in the impression formation task. When the noun is given, those adjectives still available will be processed to a semantic level. At this stage, however, time is short: only four seconds are available for semantic coding and impression formation. Semantic elaborations—even if desirable in view of subsequent recall performance—are thus impossible. Therefore, subjects in Experiment I and Experiment II process the descriptions to similar levels and show accordingly similar recall. Such an explanation may be empirically explored by giving a new group with an intention to learn *more time for semantic elaboration.*

The suggestion that more semantic elaboration is attempted when recall also is requested has one rather special implication. In our discussion of what sort of data to use, it was maintained that the inclusion of the impression formation task would secure processing of meaning. If only rather superficial processing is all that is required to form the impression in this study, however, it is very reasonable to ask to what extent this task actually has secured more "normal" processing. An impression formation task requiring something more than an evaluative judgement would most probably have been better in this respect.

The final question concerning the relationship between the conceptual framework of Craik and Lockhart and our results concerns the impact of serial position of adjectives upon recall. Are the serial position curves from the present study also compatible with such a framework?

Let us, before proceeding to a discussion of details, make a general reservation. Our discussion of serial position will to a large extent be based upon the curves shown in Figs. 5 and 6, p. 90. It may be questioned, however, how much confidence can be attributed to these curves because specific adjectives have been tied to specific positions, a point which has been discussed in more detail earlier, p. 89. This uncertainty should be kept in mind whenever reference is made to Figs. 5 and 6. The reservation is only of relevance when the serial position curves from this study are compared with those from other studies, though. When comparing serial position curves *within this study*, in which the very same stimulus material has been used, we are on safer ground.

In Noun-first conditions the adjectives were assumed to be processed rather deeply at once. The difference in storage time for the different adjectives should accordingly be of minor importance because of the resultant stability of the memory trace. We observe that the serial position curves for Noun-first conditions actually fit such expectations, showing little effect of position (Figs. 5 and 6, p. 90).

Again the situation is different in Noun-end conditions. If all five adjectives cannot be recirculated, it may be suggested that *they loose attention in the same order as they have been presented*. Such a conjecture is supported by data from Peterson and Peterson (1959), showing that the longer an item had to be stored, the greater would be the chance to be lost. Consequently—in our case—the longer an adjective must be stored, the greater should be the chance that it will be lost. The first adjective should thus be forgotten more often than the second adjective, which again should be forgotten more often than the third, and so on. The serial position curves for Noun-end conditions fit nicely such expectations (Figs. 5 and 6, p. 90).

At first sight then, the recall data appear to fit nicely with the tentative theoretical model. The empirical support from the differential effect of position is rather indirect, however. When relating decoding strategies to memory processes, attention has been directed towards each particular description in an attempt to understand in detail how that particular description is processed. The recall data used as empirical support, on the other hand, are gathered *after presentation of all six descriptions*. If memory processes relate to decoding strategies in the way suggested above, *similar serial position curves should also be found when the recall test is given immediately after each description*. A search for empirical evidence in other experiments may be revealing.

8.3.3. SERIAL POSITION CURVES FOR IMMEDIATE RECALL

In the impression formation study by Anderson and Hubert (1963), recall was required in addition to impression formation in some conditions. In every case except one, the subjects were warned of the recall task to come. The recall task was always given immediately following the formation of an impression. The serial position curves obtained in this study should therefore be of great interest. As the subjects always knew that a person was being described, moreover, the results must be compared to those of Noun-first descriptions.

The serial position curves found show the usual bowed form obtained for free recall (see, for example, Deese and Kaufman, 1957; Murdock, 1962) with both primacy and recency effects. The relative importance of these effects depends on the number (eight or six) of descriptive adjectives used. In the case of intentional recall, the curve for eight adjectives had a rather modest primacy effect. The primacy for recall of six adjectives was more pronounced, yet smaller than the recency effect. The only test of incidental recall was carried out on a set of eight adjectives. This curve also showed a modest primacy and a much stronger recency effect.

At first hand, then, it seems as if the study of Anderson and Hubert provides evidence *against* similar form of serial position curves for immediate and postponed recall. It is, however, somewhat difficult to interpret the results of the Anderson and Hubert study. In their own terminology the serial position curve give information about "verbal memory for the adjectives just heard". This memory is supposed to be distinct from the memory processes involved in impression formation, which certainly are the memory processes of primary interest in this connection. According to Anderson and Hubert, then, the information revealed in the immediate serial position curve is actually of no immediate relevance to the formation of impressions.

Such a conclusion, however, has to be modified in view of our preceding discussion of memory traces and levels of processing. The serial position curve of Anderson and Hubert is similar to the ordinary bowed serial position curve found for free recall. In the store terminology, such curves are frequently explained by suggesting that *both STS and LTS mechanisms have been involved* (see, for example, Atkinson and Shiffrin, 1968; Glanzer, 1972). The recency effect is explained by suggesting that the last elements are still in STS, while the recall of the rest of the elements is dependent on these being transferred to LTS. Craik and Lockhart (1972) explain the form of the serial position curve as the outcome of a strategy by which the first elements are processed to deeper semantic levels in order to be retained when the subjects know it will be impossible to attend to every item, or recirculate every item, on a phonemic level. The last items, on the other hand, may only be processed to phonemic levels because such coding gives excellent recall when the items are to be recalled immediately.

The first part of the serial position curve, then, should provide information bearing directly upon the formation of impressions in that semantic coding has been performed for these items. As for the recency part of the curve, the situation is more problematic. In the case of Anderson and Hubert (*ibid.*) the subjects had already given information about their impressions when the recall test was given. Every adjective should therefore have been processed to some semantic level. If not, we would have to conclude that impressions are formed exclusively on the basis of the first part of the information presented. In order to solve the problem of the recency effect, then, we may conjecture that the subject's capacity for processing may be diverted between recirculating the last words at a specific, probably phonemic, level and processing these same words to deeper levels. In some discussions of STS/LTS, a similar position is adopted. Atkinson and Shiffrin (1968), for example, explicitly suggest that material may be transferred into LTS and also continue to exist in STS.

If we assume that processing capacity is diverted, a direct comparison between the serial position curves from the Anderson and Hubert study and the present one is questionable because the former are presumedly strongly influenced by elements still recirculated at a phonemic level. It is, however, possible to circumvent the possibility of phonemic recirculation and still gain information about rather immediate recall. In connection with free recall of lists of words, the influence of elements recirculated at a phonemic level (or still in STS) is eliminated by giving an intervening task which prevents recirculation between presentation and request for recall. Such a procedure is used by Postman and Phillips (1965). They compare serial position curves of lists composed of 10, 20 or 30 words for different retention intervals. The intervals used were 0 seconds, 15 seconds and 30 seconds. In the retention interval the subjects were required to count backwards in steps of three. The serial position curves found for the 0 seconds intervals (which is the ordinary free recall situation) had the usual bowed form with primacy and recency effects. With a retention interval of 15 seconds, the recency effect was greatly reduced. Some traces of it were still left, however, especially in the shorter lists. When the retention interval was prolonged to 30 seconds, all recency effects seemed to have disappeared. Comparable results have also been reported by Glanzer and Cunitz (1966).

The results of Postman and Phillips pertain to lists of unconnected words and it may be questioned to what extent they are relevant for our descriptions. Alice Katagiri (1969), however, used essentially the same procedure in the experiment referred to earlier (p. 113). Her stimulus material was rather similar to that used in the present experiment. Since

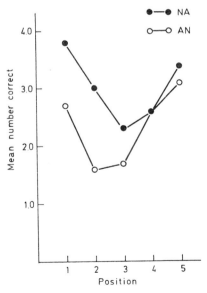

Fig. 12. Serial position curves from the study by Katagiri (after Katagiri, 1969).

her results have not been published, the resultant serial position curves for Noun-first and Noun-end conditions are reproduced in Fig. 12.

The curve for the Noun-first condition (NA) still shows a bowed form. It is interesting to notice, however, that the recency effect is supressed in comparison with the curves obtained by Anderson and Hubert. In their case, the recency effect was greater than the primacy effect, and this is no longer the case. The direction of the change is in good correspondence with the results of Postman and Phillips. As already mentioned, information about retention interval is not given by Katagiri. It is therefore possible that her recency effect would have been further supressed if the task of counting backwards by threes had been somewhat prolonged.

The information concerning serial position curves for immediate recall referred to above, however, is not conclusive. The curves obtained in the study by Anderson and Hubert are contaminated by items which still may be recirculated at a phonemic level, and even the curve based upon Katagiri's data may be contaminated in the same way. In addition, the last curve stems from a situation where only recall was asked for. We may tentatively conclude, however, that *the more immediate curve*, uncontaminated by items still recirculated at a phonemic level, *seems to be a curve with some primacy effect, but with the recency effect leveled out.* That is, the general form of this curve approximates the form of the curve found for postponed recall at least in Experiment I (Fig. 5, p. 90).

The latter statement warrants some further comments, since actually no statistically significant effects of position were found for Noun-first conditions (Table 5, p. 93). In absolute terms, however, a primacy effect was obtained in Experiment I. According to the model of Craik and Lockhart, however, no effects of position ought to be found since every word should be processed rather immediately to similar levels. The relationship between Experiments I and II is of relevance in this connection. In the latter case, there is not even a tendency towards primacy effect. The difference between Experiments I and II may possibly be explained by reference to an experiment by Crowder (1969) to be discussed in more detail on p. 133. Crowder suggests that primacy effect is contingent upon the adoption of an active strategy by the subjects. When a more passive strategy could be assumed, the primacy effect was not observed. A more active strategy is very likely adopted by the subjects when they are informed about the recall task to come, and a request for recall has been included in all the experiments yielding primacy effects. It seems thus consistent with Crowder's results that a primacy effect turns out in Experiment I where information about the recall task was initially given, and that no primacy effect is found in Experiment II where the recall task was given without prior warning.

In summary then, our hypotheses concerning memory processes and decoding strategy seem reasonable in view of the serial position curves in our Noun-first conditions and circumstantial evidence from related studies.

The problems concerning decoding strategy and serial position curves from immediate versus postponed recall in Noun-end conditions are somewhat different, but the most immediately relevant experimental evidence stems again from the study by Katagiri (1969) and from studies of free recall of lists of words (for example Deese and Kaufman, 1957; Murdock, 1962). Katagiri found a bowed serial position curve for Noun-end conditions as well as for Noun-first conditions (cf. Fig. 12, p. 130). Only recall was asked for in the experiments referred to above, however.

We may argue that the storing of the five adjectives until the noun is given, is rather similar to the storing of other unstructured elements frequently used in free recall tasks. If so, the results of the latter type of experiments would be of immediate relevance, and we should expect a bowed serial position curve for immediate recall of the five adjectives used in a description. The bowed form has been explained by suggesting that elements at different positions are processed to different levels at the time of testing for recall. The first elements have been processed to semantic levels, while the last elements are still only processed to a phonemic level. However, this might only be the case in tasks simply asking for recall, and not in tasks asking for impression formation.

It is questionable whether decoding strategies adopted in traditional memory experiments are representative of strategies adopted in ordinary verbal communication. In the former, more attention may sometimes be paid to word form while meaning processes are not elaborated as fully as usual. Decoding strategies used in memory experiments may be unrepresentative for quite the opposite reason, however. A general point about memory experiments is that the subjects are free to explore meaning to whatever extent and in whichever direction that seems to facilitate retention.

When trying to remember a list of unconnected items, it seems reasonable for a subject to attempt to process at least part of the items to semantic levels in order to prevent a rapid rate of forgetting. In such a case, there are no constraints as to exactly which semantic or mnemonic explorations are engaged in. When storing adjectives while waiting for the noun in a situation in which an integrated meaning is presupposed and requested, the problems are different. The best procedure may then simply be to process the adjectives to a phonemic level. If a specific interpretation is ventured immediately, that interpretation may shortly afterwards prove incompatible with the subsequent parts of the phrase. The resultant confusion and retroactive modification of meaning would hamper decoding and recall.

The difference with respect to processing in the two cases may also be considered with a more explicit *communicational perspective*. The words used in the traditional memory task are not part of a communication situation, and there is hence no commitment to understand what is intended by the verbal material. The descriptions used in the impression formation task, however, are embedded in a communication situation—although a highly artificial one. Processing of words is thus constrained by the obligation to understand what is conveyed by each phrase. This obligation is induced by the very task of impression formation and the request to make known the impression by a check-mark.

But to return to the issue of memory and decoding strategy: If every adjective is processed only to phonemic level, the serial position curve should loose its primacy effect. A curve showing only recency effects, like ours, would then be expected.

The experiment by Crowder (1969) may be interpreted as lending some plausibility to such a reasoning. Crowder asked his subjects for ordered recall of 9-digit strings. In one case every string included 9 digits, in the other case these 9-digit strings were included in a set of strings with variable numbers of digits. When serial positions were examined, both primacy and recency effects were found for the sets of fixed length. When strings were unpredictable with respect to length, however, the primacy effect for the 9-digit strings almost disappeared. Crowder suggests that the subjects in the latter case adopted a more passive strategy.

The results for the unpredictable strings may be of relevance for ordinary language processing, since the length of an utterance is not ordinarily known in advance. To the extent that processing in the present experimental situation is influenced by overlearned strategies developed in normal communication, Crowder's results are thus also of relevance for our experimental situations. They would lead us to expect serial position curves without primacy effects.

However, the strategies adopted by our subjects may well have been influenced by the standard format and length of the descriptions used in the instruction, and such situationally induced sets might compete with the overlearned strategies for strings of different length. Second, Crowder used digits as stimulus material, and the processing of digits is certainly different from the processing of descriptions. Third, Noun-end descriptions may have characteristics of their own that make a direct comparison with other situations questionable. It has been suggested that active strategies give primacy effects, and that an active strategy is to be expected in tasks requiring recall. When recall is requested for Noun-end descriptions, however, no primacy effect occurs. On the contrary: the recency effect appears to become more pronounced. Thus, the similarity between intentional recall conditions is not a primacy effect, but the fact that it is the adjectives most *close to the noun* that are given a special advantage.

On the basis of the existing data, therefore, it is difficult to know what kind of more immediate serial position curve to expect in Noun-end conditions. The usual bowed serial position curves stem from situations in which only recall has been asked for. It is difficult to know how relevant such results are for experiments asking for impression formation as well. Direct interference from Crowder's study is questionable for the reasons given above. In order to gain information about immediate recall which would be of direct relevance to our particular problem, another set of experiments were therefore performed.

8.3.4. EXPERIMENT A. THE AVAILABILITY OF ADJECTIVES AT THE MOMENT THE NOUN IS PRESENTED IN NOUN-END DESCRIPTIONS

Material. In this experiment, 18 descriptions were used, each composed of five adjectives and a noun as in the main experiments. The six original descriptions were all included, and 12 additional descriptions of the same form were constructed. Sequence of adjectives was varied between A_1–A_5/A_5–A_1, an equal number of subjects receiving each order, whereas the noun always was presented at the end of the description. The material was presented by tape-recorder.

Procedure. The subjects were run in groups. They were instructed to form impressions of the entities described and asked to put a check-mark on a 7-point evaluative scale to indicate their impression. In addition, they were also informed that they might be asked to write down the five adjectives just heard on a separate sheet of paper. A special sound would indicate when recall was required. This sound was presented at the moment the noun normally would come. By use of such a signal, recall was requested for each of the six descriptions used in the main experiment. These descriptions were randomly mixed with the rest of the descriptions so that the subjects would not know when to expect the recall task.[1] In the six cases where recall was requested, no noun was presented and no impressions were asked for.

Our major aim with this study was to "enter" the decoding process just at the time the noun normally would come and find out *how many* and *which* adjectives were available at this moment. The 12 additional descriptions were included in order to secure that the decoding strategy should be characteristic of impression formation and not only geared toward recall.

Subjects. Sixteen students, 8 men and 8 women, between 20 and 30 years old participated in this experiment.

Results. The results are presented in Table 14 and Fig. 13. Table 14 shows in how many cases all five adjectives were reproduced, in how many cases four adjectives were reproduced, and so on. Total number of cases is number of subjects (16) × number of descriptions (6), that is 96. Figure 13 shows the serial position curve. For comparison, this curve is presented together with the serial position curve from the next experiment, Experiment B, and the curve for Noun-end conditions from the study by Katagiri.

In 29 out of the possible 96 cases are all five adjectives reproduced. The modal category is 4, and average number of adjectives recalled per description is 3·9. These data, then, indicate that some of the adjectives already are lost when the noun is presented—unless the reproduction task itself interferes with memory.

The curve shown in Figure 13 for Experiment A differs from those for postponed recall (see Figs. 5 and 6, p. 90). The former shows a primacy effect not found in the latter and looks very much like another variant of the bowed serial position curve for one-trial learning (Deese and Kaufman, 1957; Murdock, 1962). *The particular serial position curves*

---

1. This procedure turned out to be very much like one suggested by Anderson and Hubert, 1963, p. 386.

for postponed recall in the main experiment, then, cannot simply be explained by what happens to the adjectives before the noun is presented.

The difference between the curve for postponed recall and the serial position curve found in Experiment A, however, may be explained in different ways. When the noun is presented, all available adjectives must be processed to semantic levels in order for the impression to be

TABLE 14

Number of adjectives recalled. Experiment A

| | Number of adjectives recalled | | | | | |
	5	4	3	2	1	Σ
Number of cases	29	39	21	6	1	96

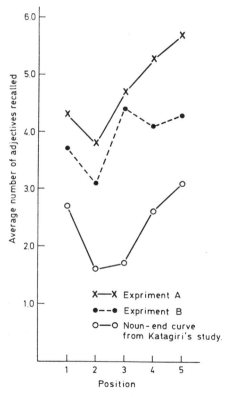

Fig. 13. Serial position curves. Experiment A, Experiment B and Noun-end curve from the study by Katagiri.

formed. Is it possible that such further processing and the impression formation *per se* might be responsible for the postponed curve, or is subsequent interference from the rest of the descriptions more important? In order to examine these possibilities, a second experiment was performed.

8.3.5. EXPERIMENT B. THE AVAILABILITY OF ADJECTIVES IMMEDIATELY AFTER IMPRESSION FORMATION

Material. In this experiment, the six descriptions of the main experiment were used once more. Sequence of adjectives was varied, an equal number of subjects receiving the adjectives in the order A_1–A_5 and A_5–A_1, whereas the noun always appeared at the end of the description. The material was again presented by means of a tape-recorder.

Procedure. The subjects were run in groups. They were instructed to form impressions of the entities described, and they were also asked to write down the adjectives of the description. For each description, the procedure was as follows: The description was presented, and the subjects were given 4 seconds to form an impression and respond with a check-mark on a 7-point evaluative scale. After 4 seconds, the noun of the description was repeated. This signalled the end of the impression formation period and served at the same time as a prompt-word for the following recall task. Thereafter, a new description was presented.

Subjects. Sixteen students, 8 men and 8 women, between 20 and 30 years old participated in this experiment.

Results. The results are given in Table 15 and Fig. 13 in a form comparable to that of the former experiment.

TABLE 15

Number of adjectives recalled. Experiment B

| | Number of adjectives recalled | | | | | | |
	5	4	3	2	1	0	Σ
Number of cases	5	42	27	17	4	1	96

Table 15 shows that the subjects were able to reproduce all 5 adjectives in only 5 out of 96 possible cases. The modal category is 4, and average number of adjectives recalled per description is only 3·25.

The resultant serial position curve is again different from the serial position curves shown in Figs. 5 and 6 for Noun-end conditions. The primacy effect from Experiment A is replicated. The serial position curve for postponed recall cannot, therefore, be fully explained by what happens when the adjectives are processed to semantic levels and impressions are formed. Subsequent processing of other descriptions also apparently influences the form of this curve.

When comparing the curves from Experiments A and B, it should be noticed that recall in the latter experiment is poorer for every position. This is particularly pronounced for the last two positions.

The effects of serial position in immediate recall of adjectives for Noun-end descriptions have now been explored at some length, and we should therefore be in a position to conclude the discussion of memory processes and decoding strategies.

8.3.6. DECODING STRATEGIES AND MEMORY PROCESSES. CONCLUDING REMARKS

The discussion of the relationship between decoding strategies and memory processes for Noun-first descriptions has already been concluded. The immediate serial position curve seems by and large compatible with the hypothesized relationship between memory processes and decoding strategies.

More problems were encountered in our Noun-end descriptions, however. The serial position curves for immediate recall all shows primacy effects (Fig. 13, p. 136). A primacy effect is observed whether the recall test is given when the noun normally should come (Experiment A), or immediately following the impression formation task (Experiment B), or postponed for a short period filled with an irrelevant task (Katagiri's study). Although the observed primacy effect in the two former experiments is not too impressive, its recurrence under three different experimental conditions cannot be ignored. It cannot simply be explained away as an artifact. If processing does not proceed beyond phonemic levels, moreover, only recency effects would be expected. How, then, are the immediate serial position effects to be interpreted?

Let us first assume that the bowed form of the serial position curve for free recall is explained by postulating that words in different positions have been processed to different levels. The primacy effect occurs because the first words are processed to semantic levels, while the recency effect is due to the fact that the last words are processed to phonemic levels only.[1]

The serial position curve from Experiment A with absolutely immediate recall, may be explained as suggested above. The primacy effect may be interpreted as evidence that *some processing to semantic levels has taken place before the noun is given.*

The assumption about adjectives being processed only to phonemic levels and then being recirculated, must be modified. If we interpret the curve literally, however, processing to a semantic level seems to pertain to only the very first adjective. The serial position curve for the last four adjectives fits nicely expectations about processing to phonemic levels. The probability that a word is forgotten increases the longer it must be recirculated.

But what can "processing to semantic levels" mean in this case? It has been maintained that the adjectives in Noun-end conditions must be stored in one way or another until the noun is given, because it is difficult to know more specifically what is conveyed by a particular adjective until one knows *what* is being characterized by it. The adjectives must hence be stored in such a way that they remain open towards different specifications at a latter stage. Phonemic storing would provide for such openness. But the same might also be true of some kind of preliminary semantic processing.

Word meaning has in this monograph been conceptualized as a process evolving over time. The initial phases of meaning processing may possibly involve very rough decisions or discriminations, leaving open possibilities for further processing. The word BIG, for example, may be immediately decoded as "big" in contrast to "little". The more specific "bigness" of BIG, however, may at such a stage still remain open. A BIG NEEDLE is much smaller than A LITTLE HOUSE. Further processing of BIG may take place as more relevant information is given. The initial processing suggested here is thus consistent with what we have maintained earlier about word autonomy (See p. 53).

In the particular context of the present experiments in which the subjects are required to rate their impressions on an evaluative scale, the positive/negative dimension of words may also become very important. As a consequence, decisions concerning how positive a specific adjective is may also be taken rather immediately, i.e. at a stage before

1. It must be noticed, however, that bowed serial position curves of course can not always be explained in such a way. See, for example, Tzeng (1973).

referential specification is achieved, whenever such a preliminary assessment of a global emotive aspect is possible.

If the above explanation of the bowed serial position curve is accepted, we have to assume that meaning processing only takes place for the first adjective. One specific and rather serious problem, however, is encountered if we assume that the last four adjectives are processed to phonemic levels only. If this were true, *how can the subject know when he gets the information required for final processing and organization?*

On a purely phonemic level, no specific characteristics discriminate between adjectives and nouns in the present case. It may perhaps be suggested that the identification of parts of speech constitutes part of the recognition process, and that the latter is independent of meaning. Apart from the many questions raised by the last part of the suggestion (see discussion below), such a point of view cannot solve the problems. In the descriptions used as stimulus material, a *noun* has been of focal significance as a prerequisite for final decoding of adjectives. In other situations, however, some other part of speech or syntactic constructions may be of focal significance (see Message structure, p. 159). *What is important is thus not a specific part of speech, as such, but rather some functional relationship between different elements.* In order to master such functional relationships, moreover, each element must at least be processed to some initial level of meaning.

The necessity of processing to at least some initial levels of meaning appears plausible also from another line of reasoning. As suggested by Rommetveit (1968, 1972c), the perceptual analysis of speech sounds includes testing for meaning. This means that phonemic perceptual processing is embedded in semantic processing and results of phonemic analyses are tested against criteria of meaning. If, for example, the result of a preliminary phonemic analysis gives a word incompatible with its context, further phonemic analyses will be pursued. And such testing must be conceived of as an intuitively and automatically mastered affair activated in experimental situations as well as in ordinary communication.

The last argument is clearly contradictory to assumptions about processing to "pure" phonemic levels, and our preliminary explanation of the serial position curve has hence to be reconsidered. We may, for instance, try to "transpose" the entire explanation to deeper levels. The primacy effect means that the first adjective is processed to *deeper semantic levels* than the rest of them. The four last adjectives are also processed to semantic levels, but only to "initial" semantic levels, i.e. to levels gene-rating rather shortlived memory traces. The continuity aspect of the conceptual framework of Craik and Lockhart (p. 120) opens up for this sort of reasoning.

A second possibility is more in line with the kind of reasoning we pur-sued in our discussion of the serial position curve found in the study by Anderson and Hubert (p. 129). It was then suggested that processing capacity may be divided between *recirculation of items on a phonemic level and further processing of these same items*. The recency part of the serial position curve may thus be accounted for by assuming that the last adjectives, while being further processed, are still available at a pho-nemic level.

In Experiment A, we also obtained information about the number of adjectives available at the moment when the noun is given. The average number was 3·9 adjectives. Assuming that the four last adjectives only are processed to initial semantic levels, this means that some of these adjectives are already lost when the noun is given and further semantic elaboration, generating more persistent traces, takes place. *If processing to deeper semantic levels rather immediately is the case in Noun-first conditions, and some adjectives already are lost before such processing is performed in Noun-end conditions, this serves to explain part of the difference in recall of adjectives due to position of noun.*

When recall is tested immediately after impression formation, as in Experiment B, recall is poorer for every position. This suppression, how-ever, is especially prominent for the last two positions. The difference between the two serial position curves is thus consistent with what hap-pens when an irrelevant task is given between presentation and recall. In such cases, depression or total disappearance of the recency effects are observed depending upon the duration of the irrelevant task. (Post-man and Phillips, 1965, see discussion on p. 130). In the present case, the intervening task—the formation of an impression, can hardly be considered irrelevant. It may nevertheless divert processing capacity away from recirculating the adjectives at a phonemic level, and the weaker recency effect in Experiment B is therefore to be expected.

It may be questioned whether the form of the serial position curve in Experiment B is of any importance whatsoever for the choice between the two alternative interpretations of the corresponding curve from Experiment A. As recall in Experiment B was tested immediately after impression formation, it must be assumed that every adjective at that time had been processed to more elaborate semantic levels. It seems reasonable, therefore, to expect that adjectives are being recirculated at a phonemic level at the same time as further processing takes place, and that such recirculation is very important for more immediate recall.

In summary, then, we have to abandon the initial most extreme hypotheses concerning memory processes and decoding strategies for Noun-end descriptions. It appears unreasonable that the five adjectives are processed to phonemic levels only until the noun is presented. Processing to initial semantic levels probably takes place. The recurrent primacy effects suggest that processing is somewhat deeper for the first adjectives.

The shape of the serial position curves, however, is most probably highly dependent on recirculation at a phonemic level. One point should be noted in this connection. For Noun-first descriptions we were much concerned with an immediate serial position curve uncontaminated by recirculated elements. When the noun is presented in Noun-end descriptions, however, it is important to know how many of the adjectives which remain available either by recirculation or other means. The latter number of adjectives represents the maximal input available for further processing.

The primacy effect in the immediate curves makes the general form of this curve different from the postponed curve. How can this difference be explained? The immediate serial position curves reveal *availability of adjectives* at that particular stage of processing. The postponed curves, on the other hand, may be interpreted as based on re-encoding of impressions (see below). They should hence be affected by *the direction of further processing* provided by the noun. The absence of primacy effects in the postponed curves may thus indicate that when the noun is given, "*backwards*" *processing takes place.* Although the first adjective is relatively well remembered, it may all the same be the last one to be further processed.

Our concern with *availability of adjectives* and *direction of processing* as separate, though interacting factors suggest an explanation of order effects incorporating aspects both from the explanation of Asch (1946) and also of attention mechanisms (Anderson, 1965). The serial position curve from Experiment A makes the recency effect in impression formation very reasonable. As more of the last adjectives are available when the impression is to be formed, these adjectives should also influence the impression more strongly than the first adjectives. This is an explanation of order effects supporting a proposal of the importance of attention.

If this is the only story, however, what would be the reason for the change in form between immediate and postponed curves?—A *backwards direction of further processing* is also compatible with the recency effect of impression formation, however. When the adjective most close to the noun is processed to deeper levels first, this provides a basis for an influence on the further processing of the other adjectives. The adjectives last heard may thus direct the processing of the rest of the adjectives in a fashion very much in line with the explanation offered by Asch (*ibid.*).

8.3.7. THE PROBLEM OF RE-ENCODING

The problem of re-encoding has already been mentioned in the present discussion. Craik and Lockhart (1972) maintain that people most often are concerned only with the meaning of stimuli, and that meaning is what we ordinarily remember. The results of the less deep analyses, on the other hand, are seldom important to remember. This point of view is rather consistent with that of Rommetveit *et al.* (1971). If this is the case, recall tasks very often imply *re-encoding*, i.e. conversion of retained meaning into word forms. Such re-encoding may or may not result in exactly the same verbal expression by which the meaning was conveyed in the first place. The chance that an identical verbal expression is given back, depends on different factors, such as, for example, the availability of synonymous words, or options with respect to syntactic constructions. Retrieval performance is assumed to be based upon the same sort of processing, however, whether the resultant verbal expression is identical to or somewhat different from that which was presented. The general problem of re-encoding is also pursued in research on memory for syntactic forms (Sachs, 1967; Johnson-Laird, 1970; Johnson-Laird and Stevenson, 1970; Fillenbaum, 1973).

The study by Rommetveit *et al.* (1971, also discussed on pp. 176–177) exploring processing of utterances in different contexts, was designed in such a way that certain assumptions about re-encoding could be tested. The subjects were to listen to a set of eight unrelated sentences, and their task was to reproduce these sentences as accurately as possible after every sentence had been presented. Before the presentation of each sentence, a specific "ready" signal was given. Different kinds of "ready" signals were employed to introduce one of the main experimental variables in this study. For one group, simple drawings of situations that would be appropriate contexts for the utterances were used. For a second group, simple sentences describing such situations were presented, and for a third group, different geometrical forms were used as ready signals.

The eight sentences used in the experiment were constructed in such a way as to provide for confusion between pairs of them. Paired sentences had a common message element in their first halves, but this same message element was expressed by different words. The last halves of the sentences, on the other hand, conveyed distinctively different message fragments.

Retrieval was in this study prompted in two different ways. The first halves of the sentences were in one condition presented as prompts for the remaining parts. In another condition, some word or expression roughly synonymous with some content element in the last part of the sentence, served as a prompt.

When recall performance was analysed, verbatim as well as synonymous expressions were taken into account. Rommetveit *et al.* conclude that what was remembered in this case were not the specific stimulus words, but what they call "higher-order message elements". The most unequivocal evidence for this conclusion was, in their own words (p. 53) "the very high over-all frequency of synonymous expressions in retrieval of sentence beginnings and the fact that retrieval was very successfully prompted by elements that did not appear in the stimulus utterances at all".

The present experiments were not designed to pursue problems of re-encoding and only adjectives given back in exactly the same word form have so far been taken into account in the analyses of recall. It is possible, however, to illustrate cases of re-encoding rather nicely with some of the data from the present experiments. In the description of SECRETARY, the adjective BEAUTIFUL (SKJØNN) was used, and a semantically strongly related (nearly synonymous) word LOVELY (VAKKER) appeared in the description of ACTRESS. For these two words we have analysed how many times exactly the same word form was given back and how many times synonymous words were recalled. Table 16 gives the results pooled together for Experiment I and Experiment II.

To decide which words should be counted as synonyms, the following procedure was employed. Every adjective prompted by ACTRESS and SECRETARY except those actually appearing in the stimulus material, was written down. Among these adjectives were words from other descriptions, from the examples in the instruction, as well as totally new words. Three judges were then asked to read this list of adjectives in order to mark those words which were synonymous to LOVELY when used about an ACTRESS (or to BEAUTIFUL used about a SECRE-TARY). In order to be counted as a synonym in the following analysis, at least two of the three judges had to mark the word as synonym. BEAUTIFUL, ATTRACTIVE, CHARMING, PRETTY, CAP-TIVATING, NICE, HANDSOME, ENCHANTING, FASCINAT-ING and DELIGHTFUL came out as synonyms of LOVELY. (The Norwegian words were SKJØNN, TILTREKKENDE, INNTAG-ENDE, PEN, FENGSLENDE, SØT, FLOTT, BEDÅRENDE, FOR-TRYLLENDE and DEILIG). LOVELY, PRETTY, ATTRACTIVE, DAINTY, NICE and CHARMING came out as synonyms of BEAU-TIFUL. (The Norwegian words were in this case VAKKER, PEN, TILTREKKENDE, YNDIG, SØT and DEILIG.)

TABLE 16

Number of adjectives given back in exactly the same word form and as synonyms to VAKKER and SKJØNN

Words presented	Words reproduced		
	Same word form	Synonyms	
LOVELY (VAKKER)	70	65	135
BEAUTIFUL (SKJØNN)	16	80	96
	86	145	

Table 16 shows that when LOVELY was presented, there were about as many instances of verbatim recall as of synonyms. For BEAUTIFUL, on the other hand, there is a very strong tendency to reproduce synonymous words. Table 17 shows match and mismatch from presentation to recall just for LOVELY and BEAUTIFUL. The results from Experiments I and II are again pooled together.

TABLE 17

Reproduction of VAKKER and SKJØNN when VAKKER
and when SKJØNN had been presented

Words presented	Words reproduced		
	LOVELY	BEAUTIFUL	
LOVELY (VAKKER)	70	22	92
BEAUTIFUL (SKJØNN)	41	16	57
	111	38	

Table 17 shows clearly that irrespective of whether LOVELY or
BEAUTIFUL appeared in the original description, LOVELY is the
one most likely to be reproduced, and such results are difficult to explain
if word forms are what is remembered. On a phonemic level LOVELY
(VAKKER) and BEAUTIFUL (SKJØNN) are very different. Reproduction must hence be conceived of as a process of re-encoding of
meaning into word form. The very same process of re-encoding must
also be assumed, however, for the reproduction of LOVELY in cases
where LOVELY really was presented. In such cases, however, it so
happens that the process of re-encoding "hits" the initial stimulus
word form.

8.3.8. THE RELATIONSHIP BETWEEN IMPRESSION FORMATION DATA AND
RECALL DATA

Impression formation and recall data have so far largely been discussed
separately. The relationship between order effects in these two sets of
data is also of interest, however, and will now be explored in some
detail.

Experiments I and II in the present study reveal considerable correspondence between impression formation and *postponed* recall. In Noun-
first conditions rather weak order effects were displayed. A tendency
towards primacy effects was observed in both sets of data in Experiment
I, however. In Noun-end conditions, on the other hand, the order effects

were more pronounced, and this proved to be the case both for impression formation and recall. Order effects in Experiment I, furthermore, is consistently stronger than those displayed in Experiment II.

A similar correspondence between the two sets of data was also obtained in the Louvain study (Jaspars *et al.*, 1971) and in the study by Luchins (1966a). A recency effect was observed in the impression formation data both for Noun-first and Noun-end descriptions in the former study, and the recall data also showed recency effects for both sets of descriptions. The unexpected recency effect in impression formation in Noun-first conditions was thus actually accompanied by a recency effect in the recall data as well.

A number of experiments were performed by Luchins (*ibid.*) to test order effects in impression formation, and a recall task was included in one of these experiments (Experiment II). Although only one continuous description, composed of an "extrovert" and an "introvert" paragraph of a person named Jim, was used in this case, the recall task is still to be considered postponed. The subjects were to give rather detailed information about their impressions in the form of a written paragraph about Jim as well as by choice of those particular words and phrases within a more inclusive set, they felt best would characterize that boy. The recall task was in this case to finish three uncompleted sentences on the basis of what they had read about Jim.[1] A primacy effect was then observed in the impression formation data, and a corresponding primacy effect was also displayed in the recall data in that the sentences mostly were completed with information from the first part of the initial description of Jim.

Some comments should also be devoted to the relationship between impression formation and *immediate* recall, particularly because Anderson and Hubert (1963) emphasize *non-correspondence* between the two sets of data. In addition to their study, Experiment B in the present monograph, is of relevance in this connection. Anderson and Hubert's study is of relevance for Noun-first conditions, while our Experiment B concerns Noun-end conditions.

In cases where both immediate recall and impression formation data

1. The material was in this case presented in written form to the subjects, and we have earlier commented upon the lack of control over the reader's sequence of information intake. Since the description of Jim was composed of one paragraph given introvert characteristics and another paragraph presenting extrovert characteristics, however, it seems reasonable to expect that the introvert-extrovert information was read in the order supposed by the experimenter.

are available, instances of both *correspondence* and *non-correspondence* can be found. In the study by Anderson and Hubert one instance of *non-correspondence* and one instance of *correspondence* were actually observed. For one description where incidental recall was tested, a *primacy* effect could be inferred for impression formation while a *recency* effect was observed in the recall data. For a set of descriptions with intentional recall, however, *recency effects were observed for impression formation as well as for recall*. The instance of non-correspondence is rather thoroughly discussed by the authors, whereas the instance of correspondence is not given much attention at all.

The recall results from Experiment B in the present monograph reveal a dominant recency effect. When impression formation data from these subjects are analysed, the results are somewhat unclear. Three descriptions show recency effects and three descriptions primacy effects. The recency effects observed, however, are of a much greater magnitude than the primacy effects. Thus, when averaging over all descriptions, the outcome is a recency effect comparable in magnitude to those observed in Experiment I.

Only 16 subjects participated in this experiment, and only eight subjects received each order of adjectives. To the extent that any conclusion can be drawn at all from such a small sample, however, the results of Experiment B also point in the direction of correspondence between impression formation and immediate recall.

The systematic correspondence between order effects in impression formation and *postponed* recall deserves closer attention. When postponed recall is re-considered in terms of *re-encoding*, such a correspondence seems to have one rather interesting implication of general interest: What is "taken out" to be remembered of the description is its meaning, that is *the impression formed*. This impression, or, more exactly, what is remembered of this impression, function as the basis for re-encoding at the time of recall. The correspondence in structure between *the recall data* and *the impression immediately formed* suggests that the intervening stage—*the impression remembered*, also has this same general structure.

This point bears on our previous discussion of what sort of data to use. It was noted that memory data in many cases seemed indirect and also involved a number of problems because it was difficult to know what happened in the period of memory. If the immediate impression and the impression remembered have the same general structure, however, this provides evidence in support of use of recall data in studies of impression formation and decoding strategies.

8.4. Integration of the descriptions

In this part, issues concerning integration of the descriptions will be taken up. The term integration will be used to refer to *the process of integration*. The "result" of this integration, what might be called *the structure of the final impression* will also be explored, however. It is of interest first of all because it may throw further light on the process of integration, but also in its own right. Thus, relationships between *dynamic processing* and *static cross-cuts* at specific points in time will have to be spelled out.

Problems of integration were also encountered in the discussion of the relation between decoding strategies and memory processes. The present discussion aims at a further explication of the same issues. We suggested that integration is related to level of semantic elaboration (p. 126), but this point needs some further clarification. We shall also explore the concept of integration with the hope that it may contribute more to the explanation of differences in recall than what has been suggested so far. And we shall finally explore the structure of the impressions and examine whether such structural analysis may provide additional clues to the process by which final impressions are generated.

8.4.1. INTEGRATION AND SEMANTIC ELABORATION

The differential effect of instruction in Noun-first and Noun-end conditions has been related to the possibility for further semantic elaboration and integration in the intentional learning situation only for Noun-first conditions (p. 126). The explanation is based on the assumption that the subjects attempt to integrate as a mean to promote recall, and implies that further semantic processing then is a prerequisite. As the impression formation task as such also requires integration, this implies that integration or the linking together of words presented separately, is not an all or none affair. The meanings of these separate words may become linked into a more or less closely organized whole.

In order to explore in more detail the relationship between integration and further semantic processing, we have to ask what is implied by the idea that the meanings of different words become integrated or linked together. One possible interpretation is that the meaning processes of the separate words gradually lose their *separateness* or *discreteness*. The meaning processes becomes more and more integral components of *one process*, and in such a way that it becomes artificial to talk about the meaning processing of one word as distinct from meaning processing of another. This is so because the meaning processing of one word is *influenced by* or dependent upon the meaning processing of the others.

The dependency among words is part and parcel of the more general conception of words as open and dynamic (Part I). What is of interest from a communication perspective is clearly what the sender wants to convey by the words jointly. This holds also for our impression formation task: Forming an impression means comprehending what the whole description conveys.

According to this chain of reasoning, the discreteness of words is gradually lost as further processing takes place. Word meaning was conceptualized as an act of reference followed by a representational, an emotive, and an associative component. The initial phase of such processing may be discrete in some sense. It may be related to the autonomy of the word, and may not be very much influenced by context. The adjectives in Noun-end descriptions may thus be processed to an initial semantic level, although it is at that stage not yet known which entity they characterize. For further processing, however, such information becomes necessary.

To illustrate, the phrase A BEAUTIFUL SECRETARY, may be pursued through gradually more elaborate semantic processing. When only BEAUTIFUL is heard, it may rather promptly be understood in an abstract, yet undetermined fashion as opposed to UGLY. For further processing, however, more information is required. BEAUTIFUL said about a SECRETARY differs from BEAUTIFUL referring to, e.g. MUSIC. In the former case the word conveys aesthetic aspects of three dimensional human bodies while reference in the latter case has to do with temporal configurations of sounds. The processing of BEAUTIFUL is thus "coloured" by the noun to which it is connected from the very moment such a connection is established. Still more "colouring" is to be expected with more time to pursue the processing. The latter may lead to increased specificity and be directed toward one particular secretary known to the receiver. In order to be congruent with the qualifying adjective, this real-life secretary has to be beautiful in one way or another. That is, BEAUTIFUL influences possible experiental specification or anchoring of SECRETARY, and vice versa. BEAUTIFUL, in turn, may be elaborated in the direction of the unique beauty of this very same person. The processing of one word is thus interwoven with the processing of the other to such an extent that it may be questioned if the two processes any longer can be disentangled. In other words, A BEAUTIFUL SECRETARY has at that stage been rather well integrated.

Integration may also be discussed from another perspective, however. It may be explored in terms of visual imagery. Such a point of view is of particular relevance in our experimental context since the nouns used in our descriptions were rather concrete.

Lambert and Paivio (1956, p. 9) suggest that the superiority of noun-adjective over adjective-noun order is related to the use of the noun "as a conceptual 'peg' from which its modifiers can be hung". The notion of the noun as a conceptual "peg" has also been advocated in more recent studies (Paivio, 1963; Kusyszyn and Paivio, 1966; Yuille, Paivio and Lambert, 1969). In these latter studies, it has been maintained that the efficiency of the noun as a conceptual "peg" is related to its capacity to elicit imagery which in turn mediates recall.

To integrate seems thus according to this view to imply that what is mediated by some words, most probably the adjectives, are connected to the image generated by some other word—probably the noun— functioning as a memory peg. Such a connection of words to an image may perhaps most plausibly be interpreted as involving the creation of a compound image by which the characteristics conveyed by every word involved is simultaneously illustrated.

The imagery approach to integration, however, will not be further pursued here. Much of our subsequent discussion might fit within such a frame. We shall focus upon processing of meaning primarily from the general perspective outlined in Part I, however, and how an imagery approach may be incorporated in such a general framework, will not be discussed.

When integration is discussed in terms of word meaning processing or formation of imagery, we explicitly adopt an approach which can be characterized as *intentional*. Another possible approach, however, would be to focus on *extensional* criteria. Our descriptions are endo-centric constructions in that the combination of words denotes a subset of the denotatum of one of the content words included. To illustrate, the denotatum of A SEVERE SECRETARY falls within the denotatum of SECRETARY. More specifically, it may be said to denote an inter-section of the denotata of SECRETARY and SEVERE, and each adjective in a description thus serves to reduce the denotative extension of the noun. That a description is integrated may hence be taken to mean that the subject *knows*, or has identified, or is in one way or another *directed towards* the denotatum of the resultant combination of words.

Dependency among words, however, must also be taken into con-sideration in this connection. It is often the case that the denotatum of one given word is influenced by some other content words belonging to the same phrase. The denotatum of RED, for instance, will most probably have somewhat different extensions when used to characterize, e.g. hair colour or colour of dresses. The colour appropriately labelled RED in the former case would probably often be labelled ORANGE in the latter context.

An extentional perspective, moreover, has little to offer in terms of explication of decoding processes and explanation of differences in recall and will not be given further consideration.

8.4.2. INTEGRATION AND THE SUPERIORITY OF NOUN-FIRST

The question was raised whether differences with respect to memory involved in *initial decoding* of descriptions may explain the substantial differences in recall of adjectives between Noun-first and Noun-end descriptions. We found, then, that only approximately four out of five adjectives would be available for deeper processing in the Noun-end conditions. The effect of this early loss of one adjective may be estimated, moreover, if we assume that percentage loss of adjectives would be the same whether four or five adjectives per description were subjected to more elaborate processing. The average number of adjectives recalled from Noun-end descriptions per subject is approximately 5·6.[1] If five adjectives were subjected to more elaborate processing, recall perfor-mance should rise to 7·0 adjectives per subject. The lowest number of adjectives recalled per person in Noun-first descriptions, however, was 8·7.[2] Such an estimate of recall performance seems therefore to imply that other factors than initial memory loss must have been of impor-tance as well.

1. Averaging over the results from Experiments I and II, Appendix D. Tables D1 and D2.
2. Experiment II, Appendix D. Table D2.

The latter conclusion is also strongly supported by the data from the Louvain study (Jaspars *et al.*, 1971). *In the latter, only four adjectives were used in the descriptions.* Although every adjective therefore most probably was available for further processing at the moment when the noun was given, the difference in recall performance between Noun-first and Noun-end conditions was still very substantial.

We may hence, in our attempt to account for the rather striking difference in recall, examine more closely the *possibility to integrate the descriptions in Noun-first and Noun-end descriptions.* A differential opportunity for integration was already included as part of our preliminary models of decoding strategies: A cumulative decoding strategy implies a continuous possibility to integrate, and only one adjective has to be handled at a time. A postponed strategy, on the other hand, implies that integration must await further information. Once the noun is made known, moreover, the subjects have simultaneously to integrate and keep available adjectives. This may exceed the processing capacity, and some adjectives may be lost also at this stage. The difference in recall of adjectives between Experiments A and B is consistent with such an explanation. A rather clear account of subjective experience of integration difficulties in Noun-end descriptions was given by one of our subjects:

> One reason why it is so difficult to form a picture of these expressions, is the fact that the noun (BOOK, SCULPTURE and so on) was given at the end. As a consequence, one knew in just a few seconds what all these adjectives were about. Because of this, the collection of adjectives becomes rather detached and the connection is understood a bit too late.

In this case, images seem to have been elicited. Whether or not this was so, however, is not important. The main point, the problem of establishing connections or understanding relationships, remains whether imagery is involved or not.

The differential effects of instruction in Noun-first and Noun-end conditions, moreover, also testify to the problems of integration in the latter conditions. The subjects have to use all their capacity to perform the impression formation task and cannot manage further semantic elaboration and integration although such activities most probably would yield recall benefits.

Lack of integration is also revealed in what might be called "loose" adjectives. When scoring recall, only adjectives given back in response to *correct prompt word* were counted as correct. However, we also counted every adjective reproduced *disregarding whether it was given back in response to correct or incorrect prompt word*. The difference between these two scores is significantly greater for Noun-end descriptions than for Noun-first descriptions (p. 95).

8.4.3. INTEGRATION AND THE STRUCTURE OF THE IMPRESSIONS

So far, we have discussed the process of integration in rather general terms, and little has been said more specifically about patterns of dependencies among words. The latter should in part be revealed in the structure of the impressions formed as this is mirrored in the recall data. What, then, can be said about this structure?

Its main characteristic is the focal significance of the noun. This was assumed in our initial models of decoding strategies and is strongly supported by the recall data. The focal position of the noun is also corroborated in more specific analyses.

We have seen, first of all, that the noun functions significantly better than the first adjective as prompt word for the adjectives at positions 2, 3 and 4 (p. 97). This is true both for Noun-first and Noun-end descriptions. The noun thus seems to convey information of more central strategic importance in retrieval of the entire description than what is the case for the first adjective.

When *first adjective* was used as prompt word, retrieval of noun was far superior to retrieval of any single adjective (Fig. 11, p. 98). The recall of the noun at the end of descriptions was thus more than twice as good as that of the neighbouring adjective (0·9 versus 0·4) for Noun-end descriptions.

The relationship between *noun* and *first adjective*, moreover, is asymmetrical, and more clearly so for Noun-first descriptions. When the *noun* was given as prompt word in this case, an average of 1·8 of the six possible first adjectives was remembered. When the *first adjective* served as a prompt, however, the average recall of nouns was 3·3. In this case. the backward "association" is thus definitely the stronger one. The corresponding numbers from Noun-end descriptions were 0·7 and 0·9.

The central importance of the noun is also cogently demonstrated by additional, more detailed analysis of retrieval prompted by adjectives. When *first adjective* served as a prompt, the subjects sometimes reproduced a wrong noun. We hence made a special analysis of the other *adjectives* given back in these cases, and it turned out that *almost seven times as many of these adjectives belonged to the description from which the "wrong" noun had been retrieved than to the description of the adjective prompt word* (Table 9, p. 101). This testifies to a rather unequivocal strategy of retrieval: The subjects try first of all to "reach" the appropriate noun, and then, *via that noun*, the remaining adjectives.

A similar conclusion is arrived at by Jaspars *et al.* (1971, p. 123), when analysing the extent to which adjectives were recalled in combination. They write:

> This means that in both conditions, the associations between adjectives are completely determined by the associations between the adjectives and the noun and no evidence has been found for a cumulative mechanism beyond such a noun-adjective linkage.

The quotation above, however, should not be interpreted too literally. The experimental set-up both in our experiments and in the Louvain study is such that "connections" *between adjectives* in many cases compete with a connection *between adjective and noun*. When the latter wins, it is only implied that this connection is the stronger one, *not* that no connection whatsoever exists between adjectives. In what follows, however, we shall pay major attention to the stronger and more salient noun-adjective connection.

The structure of impressions can thus be characterized as one in which the noun is central and where comparatively weak direct connections—if any at all—seem to exist between adjectives. This is so both for Noun-first and Noun-end descriptions. One feature distinguishes these structures, however. The serial position of the adjective has little influence in Noun-first description, and every adjective seems thus to be equally well connected to the noun. For Noun-end descriptions, on the other hand, clear effects of adjective position are revealed so that adjectives at different positions differ with respect to strength of connection to the noun.

Our preliminary models of decoding strategies for Noun-first and Noun-end descriptions were said to be ambiguous in that they may depict *structures* as well as *processes* (see Fig. 1, p. 58). What makes them ambiguous, is that the left–right connections can be used to illustrate *topological relations between elements* and/or *the dimension of time*. If these figures now are to be interpreted purely as topological structures, however, how do they compare to those suggested by the recall data?

The structure of the impression for Noun-first descriptions indicated by the recall data differs from the initial model. In the latter, only the first adjective is connected directly to the noun. Later adjectives are tagged onto *a noun already modified*. On the basis of the initial model, we should thus expect a clear effect of position. The reason is simply that the prompt word (the noun) should differ more and more from the complex (the modified noun) to which the adjective is directly linked as we proceed from A_1 to A_5. Such expectations are not corroborated by our findings. If a structure of the impression is depicted on the basis of our recall data, Fig. 14 may serve as an approximation of that of the Noun-first descriptions.

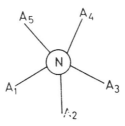

Fig. 14. The structure of the impression in Noun-first descriptions.

The empirically inferred structure of impressions for Noun-end descriptions shares some of the characteristics depicted in Fig. 14, since *central importance of the noun* as well as *weak connections between adjectives* are common for both structures. If we want to take into account variations with respect of strength of connections, however, a structure such as the one depicted in Fig. 15 seems more appropriate. The length of the lines between noun (N) and adjective (A) mirrors the strength of connection: The longer the line, the weaker the connection. This structure also differs from the structure suggested in Fig. 1, in part because the latter may be interpreted as indicating strong connections between adjectives.

Figures 14 and 15 are based on group data, but individual recall of any single word is an all-or-none affair. If we consider retention as a continuum extending below the threshold for retrieval, however, the structures in Figs. 14 and 15 may be conceived of as illustrations of modal individual structures.

When we started out discussing decoding strategies we were primarily concerned with what might be called *active processing*. In reality, however, decoding must be conceived of as a compound of active, elaborating processes and *forgetting*. The structure inferred on the basis of a cross-cut at a specific point in time is clearly a result of both aspects of processing, and the structures suggested in Figs. 14 and 15 may indeed be conceived of as generated by precisely such composite processing.

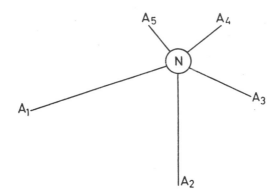

Fig. 15. The structure of the impression in Noun-end descriptions.

The lines should picture connections established during such composite processing, and it is time to consider these connections more closely. The term "connections between words" has been used so far.[1] Little has been said about the specific character of these connections, but we have suggested that they must be of a more complex nature than pure associations, perhaps such that one element serves as some sort of *presupposition* or *background* for another.

Let us assume, now, that these connections are most appropriately conceived of as such *relations of dependency* among words. If so, the structure of the final impression should provide clues to the pattern of dependencies inherent in the description, and hence to dependencies among component parts of the decoding process. Such a line of reasoning, moreover, provides one insight into more qualitative aspects of integration.

One very important characteristic of the dependency relations is *not* explicitly shown in the Figs. 14 and 15: *The relation between noun and adjective is clearly asymmetrical,* the adjective being much more dependent on the noun than vice versa. This asymmetry is cogently documented in the very substantial difference in recall performance due to noun position. If the dependency relation was symmetrical, the first adjective

1. Jaspars *et al.* use the term association (1971, p. 123).

in Noun-end condition might function very much like the noun in Noun-first condition, probably making the decoding strategies much more similar.

The pattern of dependencies, moreover, is similar in Noun-first and Noun-end descriptions despite specific differences between the two conditions with respect to processing. It must hence be conceived of as some as yet not fully identified abstract characteristic of processing, a characteristic we shall deal with at some length when we now expand the scope of analyses and adopt a general communication perspective.

9

Message Structure

The central importance of the noun within the descriptions has repeatedly been noted. Our first problem will now be to explore the generality of this phenomenon. Are our experimental results due to specific psychological characteristics of *nouns* and *adjectives*? Or is it more reasonable to expect that the results depend on *the functional relationship* between these word groups in the present descriptions, and that the experiments thus point to principles of a much more general nature? In the discussion to follow, the latter position will be defended.

The functional relationship between nouns and adjectives will be further discussed from an explicit *social psychological point of view*, and the noun and the adjective within the description will be considered instances of *free* and *bound information*, respectively (Rommetveit, 1972c, 1974). After a brief presentation of these concepts, we shall argue that the superiority of Noun-first in the present case is an example of the more general rule of the *superiority of pre-position of the free information*. In support of this position, findings from a new experiment by this author as well as from experiments by Bransford and Johnson (1973) will be reported. These experiments also serve to clarify the very notion of free versus bound information and will hence hopefully pave the way for a more thorough discussion of these concepts and the more inclusive notion of *message structure*.

9.1. Free and bound information and the superiority of Noun-first

We claimed that the noun and the adjectives within our descriptions may be considered instances of free and bound information, respectively. What, then, is *free* and *bound information*?

As a first approach, the distinction may be compared to that between free and bound *morphemes*. The bound morpheme never appears alone, but must be "bound" to some other—most often a free—morpheme. The morpheme for plural in English, for instance, cannot even be unequivocally identified in isolation. The "s" will be a different entity, semantically, depending upon whether it appears in the verb CHATS or in the noun CATS. Its semantic contribution, however, is immediately given once it is tagged on to the free morpheme, CAT.

In a similar fashion, the free information is in general defined as that part of the entire information which provides the background, or the necessary information for processing of other parts. The other parts, then, convey bound information. In our descriptions, therefore, the noun (for example: SECRETARY) serves as free information. Thus, what is conveyed by SEVERE cannot be fully determined unless it is taken for granted that, e.g. a secretary is being described.

It seems evident, therefore, that the main variation of descriptions, *Noun-first versus Noun-end, can be considered particular instances of pre-position versus post-position of free information.* It is hence reasonable to ask whether the superiority of recall of adjectives observed for Noun-first descriptions in the present study will be observed also in other cases where *free information is given first, but by other constructions than a single noun.* To explore this problem, a new experiment, Experiment C, was performed.

9.1.1. EXPERIMENT C. PRE-POSITION VERSUS POST-POSITION OF FREE INFORMATION

Material: The stimulus material consisted of eight sentences, each of which appeared in three different forms. Sentence 1 in its three forms is given below:

I WHEN THE SUN GOES DOWN, IT IS IMPRESSIVE, BEAUTIFUL AND COOL (In Norwegian: NÅR SOLEN GÅR NED, ER DET STEMNINGSFULLT, VAKKERT OG KJØLIG)[1]

II IT IS IMPRESSIVE, BEAUTIFUL AND COOL WHEN THE SUN GOES DOWN.

1. To translate these sentences from Norwegian to English involves problems. The two versions differ, and probably also with respect to a characteristic emphasized in this monograph: word openness. Thus, IMPRESSIVE, for example, has meaning potentials that cannot de conveyed by its Norwegian "equivalent" STEMNINGS-FULL.

III IMPRESSIVE, BEAUTIFUL AND COOL IS IT WHEN THE SUN GOES DOWN.

It is assumed for all three variants that the clause WHEN THE SUN GOES DOWN functions as free information. What is conveyed by COOL, for instance, is not fully known until it is taken for granted that a sunset is being talked about. Convergence of sender and receiver onto the same entity is thus a necessary prerequisite for similar processing of adjectives, the bound information. Constructions I and III exemplify the sequence *free-bound* and *bound-free* information, respectively, which is the main variable in this experiment. Construction II was included primarily for exploratory purposes. It has (as III) free information in post-position, but has in addition an introductory deictic element (IT).

In addition to sentence 1, the 7 following sentences were used. They are all presented in form I below, together with the original Norwegian versions.

2. MEETING SUCH A PERSON IS REFRESHING, EXCITING AND UNEXPECTED. (Å TREFFE ET SLIKT MENNESKE ER FORFRISKENDE, SPENNENDE OG OVERRASKENDE.)

3. WEARING SHORT SKIRTS IS PRETTY, COLD AND EASY. (Å HA KORT SKJØRT ER PENT, KALDT OG LETTVINT.)

4. IF HE IS ELECTED, IT IS FRIGHTENING, INCREDIBLE AND DEPRESSING. (HVIS HAN BLIR VALGT, ER DET SKREMMENDE, UTROLIG OG DEPRIMERENDE.)

5. THAT THE EXAM WENT WELL, IS FUN, STRANGE AND ENCOURAGING. (AT EKSAMEN GIKK BRA, ER MORSOMT, MERKELIG OG OPPMUNTRENDE.)

6. WHEN EXHIBITIONS ARE OPENED, IT IS COMICAL, UNNATURAL AND CROWDED. (NÅR UTSTILLINGER BLIR ÅPNET, ER DET KOMISK, UNATURLIG OG TRANGT.)

7. THAT THE WEATHER IS BAD, IS ANNOYING, UN-PLEASANT AND HINDERING. (AT VÆRET ER STYGT, ER KJEDELIG, VEMMELIG OG ØDELEGGENDE.)

8. TO CONFESS ONE'S DISHONESTY, IS STRAIGHT-
    FORWARD, BRAVE AND PRAISEWORTHY. (Å TILSTÅ
    SIN UÆRLIGHET ER REALT, MODIG OG ROSVERDIG.)

The sentences thus vary with respect to the syntactic form of the part conveying the free information.

The material was presented by means of a tape-recorder. A master-tape was used in the technical production of the stimulus material in a way analogous to that employed in the main experiments, and the adjective parts were thus kept identical across the three sentence forms.

Procedure: Three groups of subjects participated in the experiment. Each group heard one set of eight sentences. Every sentence within a given set was given in the same form, either in form I, II or III. The task was only to remember the adjectives, and the instruction included two practice items. Order of presentation was indicated above with 4 seconds between items. For reproduction, the subjects were given small booklets with one page for each sentence. The sentence with open spaces for the adjectives to be reproduced was given to prompt recall. The order of recall was different from the order of presentation. The subjects were allowed to proceed at their own speed in the recall task, and they were instructed never to turn back to preceding items.

Subjects: Sixty subjects participated in this experiment. They were all students in the introductory phase of their studies, and each group consisted of 10 men and 10 women.

Results: Recall of adjectives was highest for sentence form I, and lowest for III, with II in between. Average number of adjectives recalled was 12·4, 8·9 and 10·7, respectively, out of a maximum possible of 24. As shown in Fig. 16, this order holds for six out of the eight sentences, and the superiority of form I over form III holds for every sentence.

The analysis of variance reported in Table 18 shows that *the effect of sentence form* as well as *the effect of the specific sentences* are significant. The difference in recall of adjectives between the two extreme forms, I and III, is significant with $p < 0.001$ (t = 3·64, t-test for uncorrelated means).

Discussion: Also in this experiment recall is superior when free information is given first. For the extreme forms, I and III, the results are very clear. Although the sentences differ significantly from each other with respect to ease of recall and even though different constructions are used to convey the free information, recall of sentences with pre-position of free information is superior in every case. The results thus indicate that the superiority of the sequence noun-adjective in our main experiments, should be interpreted within a more general frame. The central importance of the noun is also given a new perspective. It

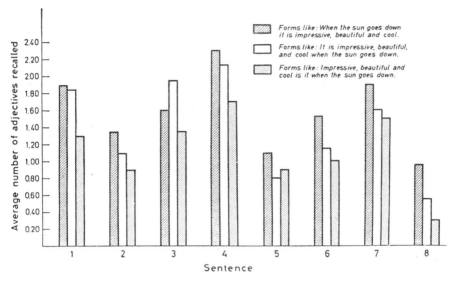

Fig. 16. Average number of adjectives recalled per sentence for the different sentence forms.

TABLE 18

Analysis of variance[1] of recall of adjectives in the three different sentence forms

Source	Sum of squares	df	Estimate	F	p
Between subjects	91·07	59			
Se. F	17·32	2	8·66	6·69	0·01
Subjects within groups	73·76	57	1·29		
Within subjects	332·13	420			
Se	95·05	7	13·58	23·41	0·001
Se. F × Se	6·88	14	0·49	0·84	
Se × Subjects within groups	230·19	399	0·58		

Se. F: Sentence form
Se: Sentence
[1] Split-plot design.

should probably *not* be attributed to its "nounness", but to the fact that it *in this case functions as free information.*

The recall for form II falls between that of form I and III respectively. Although forms II and III both are similar in that the bound information is presented ahead of the free, the particular position of IT IS thus also seems to affect processing. We may ask, therefore, whether even the rather indeterminate IT already restricts the possibilities of what is to follow. Reichling (1963) maintains that as a formal subject IT is without semantic meaning. We may argue, however, that IT implies a neuter gender (i.e. IT in contrast to HE, SHE or THEY) of what is to come. The segment IT IS may thus in the particular context of the experiment signal that *some state of affair* rather than, e.g. one or more *persons* is being talked about. One characteristic of the Norwegian language complicates this sort of reasoning, however. Some of the adjectives used in the sentences are inflected in such a way that they also imply a neuter gender of what is to come. Thus forms II and III may in some cases both be said to provide such information in the initial part of the sentence. This holds true for four of our eight sentences. However, other factors also may account for the difference between forms II and III. Form III thus seems intuitively to be the less usual one. The mere time interval filled by IS IT, intervening between the adjectives and the postponed free information in form III, moreover, may also affect processing.

9.1.2. FURTHER SUPPORT FOR THE SUPERIORITY OF PRE-POSITION OF FREE INFORMATION

In the experiments discussed so far, both free and bound information has been contained within one sentence or one description. The concepts as such, however, have a much wider range of applicability. In this section reference will be made to two experiments by Bransford and Johnson (1973) which could be interpreted within a frame of free and bound information, but where the information is given by other means. In the first of the experiments, all information is verbal in character. In the second one, however, information is mediated by both visual and verbal means. In the former experiment, the subjects were to listen to a connected passage of approximately 180 words. Although the passage contained only grammatically correct and complete sentences, it was in itself rather difficult to understand. This was the case because many of the words were general and rather undetermined with respect to reference, as for example: PROCEDURE, ARRANGE, FACILITIES, THINGS, MATERIALS, MISTAKE. Very few cues, if any, were given in the passage as to what it all was about.

Three groups of subjects participated in the experiment. One group listened to the passage only, whereas the two other groups were also informed of *the topic of the passage*. One group received this information *before* they listened to the passage, the other group was given the same information *after* having listened to the whole passage. The tasks were to give comprehension ratings for the passage and to recall as much as possible of it afterwards. The results show clearly the superiority of the *"topic before"—condition* both regarding comprehension and recall. The two other conditions were rather similar with respect to both measures.

In view of our previous tentative definition, *information about topic clearly serves as free information in this case*. A convergence with respect to topic would be required in order for efficient message transmission to take place. The experiment thus lends additional support to the superiority of pre-position as compared to post-position of free information regarding recall.

In the other experiment by Bransford and Johnson, a connected passage of approximately 130 words was used. The passage was this time also composed of grammatically correct sentences, but was again rather difficult to understand in isolation. The words were not so undetermined as in the previously described passage, however. What made this latter passage particularly hard to comprehend seemed rather to be that the situation into which it should fit was a rather novel and unusual situation. This situation was presented by way of *a visual illustration*.

The experiment included several conditions, and among these were three closely resembling those from the first mentioned experiment. One group listened to the passage only, one group was first shown the visual illustration and then read the passage, whereas the last group was given these pieces of information in the reversed order. The tasks were identical to those from the former experiments, and so were also the main trends of the results.

The picture conveys in this case information serving as background or necessary information for the comprehension of the passage. *The superiority of pre-position of free information seems thus not to be confined to situations where all the relevant information is verbal in nature*. We shall return to relationships between what is seen and what is heard later on in a discussion of the studies by Rommetveit *et al.* (1971) and Blakar and Rommetveit (1975) (p. 176).

9.2. Free and bound information and message structure

In order to account for relatively well established experimental results on recall of verbal and combined pictorial and verbal material, we have resorted to the concepts of free and bound information. We shall now consider these concepts more closely, and by doing so we shall also try to relate them to the more inclusive notion of message structure. The subsequent discussion is clearly influenced by the works of Ragnar Rommetveit. For a more extensive discussion of the key concepts, both those of primary interest in the present context and related ones, the reader is referred to his works, particularly to his book "On message structure" (1974).

9.2.1. A MORE DETAILED DISCUSSION OF FREE AND BOUND INFORMATION

The concepts of free and bound information are primarily to be understood within the framework of *language use*. They apply to communication, to the sending and receiving of messages, and to *prerequisites for making something known to another person*. These concepts are, furthermore, based upon the assumption that different parts of an utterance or of the information presented, function in different ways. This position was supported by a concrete example in the initial part (p. 32). When THE OLD MAN IS POOR is uttered in a situation like the one there described, THE OLD MAN is not used to make anything known to the receiver, but serves primarily a convergence of attention on the part of the sender and receiver towards the same man. The second part of the utterance, IS POOR, may convey what the sender intends if, and only if, this is accomplished. What is conveyed in the first part of the utterance is, in a way, supposed to be taken for granted and not open for questioning. And this unquestioned information, giving the necessary background for comprehending the remaining part as intended by the speaker, is *the free information*. What is conveyed by the remaining part, that which is *made known*, is *the bound information*.

As already examplified, the concepts of free and bound information are rather general and can be applied at different levels of analysis. At the one extreme, we may talk about free and bound morphemes. In the descriptions used in the main experiments the noun functions as free information, the adjectives as bound. The whole description, moreover, may function as free information in an expanded utterance, like the following one: A SEVERE, COOL, EXTRAORDINARY, BEAUTIFUL AND PLEASANT SECRETARY APPLIED FOR THE JOB. This utterance may in turn be expanded and inserted in a situation in such a way that all words given above would serve to convey free information. The resultant utterance might be, for example, THAT THE SEVERE, COOL, EXTRAORDINARY, BEAUTIFUL AND PLEASANT SECRETARY APPLIED FOR THE JOB, WAS JUST A LIE.

The *relative character* of free and bound information can also be illustrated with another modification of the description. Suppose, for instance, that THE SECRETARY WAS SEVERE, COOL, EXTRAORDINARY, BEAUTIFUL AND PLEASANT is uttered in response to the question: HOW WAS THE SECRETARY APPLYING FOR THE JOB? The adjective part constitutes then the novel information, that which is *made known* or *asserted* by the utterance. If, on the other hand, the question was WHO WAS SEVERE, COOL, EXTRAORDINARY, BEAUTIFUL AND PLEASANT, the noun part of the answer IT WAS THE SECRETARY WHO WAS SEVERE, COOL, EXTRAORDINARY, BEAUTIFUL AND PLEASANT constitutes what is made known. In every example, a *nesting* of free and bound information appears. What is made known is at every stage bound to whatever at that stage is assumed to be *shared knowledge*.

The analysis of free and bound information is also of relevance for still more inclusive units of verbal communication. In one of the experiments, a rather long passage was characterized as conveying bound information in relation to information concerning the topic of that passage. The latter was conceived of as free information. When specific matters are to be discussed, as for example some psychological theory as part of a student's paper, some knowledge of that theory may be characterized as free information providing the necessary background for an understanding of more specific comments.

The applicability of the distinction between free and bound information, moreover, is by no means constrained to purely verbal information. In one of the experiments referred above a picture conveyed the free information. In ordinary communication, concrete situational context may thus often provide essential parts of that information. It may indeed at times be a matter of chance by which kind of means a necessary convergence upon some entity is established. In the example of THE OLD MAN IS POOR, it is established by the use of a verbal expression. If that man happens to be within the shared visual field of the sender and receiver, a pointing gesture might function equally well. This should not be taken to imply, however, that choice of means is devoid of consequences.

The concepts of free and bound information may also be brought to bear upon relationships between that which is tacitly assumed to be the case and what is explicitly said in particular situations. How an utterance is understood is contingent upon what is reflectively or unreflectively assumed to be relevant shared knowledge. The significance of such a kind of free information may become very salient—at least to the receiver—in cases where it is lacking. This is certainly often the case when one of the participants in the act of communication is a child, as in the following example. One evening when I was putting my son, four years old, to bed, we both heard the sound of a plane. This reminded him of something, and he said: WE HAVE NOT SEEN NINA'S PLANE. The only possible common knowledge or *shared free information* I could imagine that might make this statement understandable, was that *we both knew a little girl named Nina whose father was a pilot.* My son might hence be referring to the fact that we had never seen "his" plane, I thought, but I was wrong. When such an interpretation was suggested, I was informed that Nina, who had been working in his kindergarten, was to travel by plane to England that very day.

The very general and abstract character of the notion of free versus bound information has by now, it is hoped, been documented. And let us now try to relate these concepts to the traditional concepts of *subject—predicate* and *topic—comment*.

The distinction between subject and predicate is according to Garver (1967) of relevance within the following four areas of discourse: grammar, epistemology, logic, and metaphysics. Their use within epistemology is of particular interest in this connection, and Garver describes the contrast between subject and predicate within this area as follows (*ibid.* p. 33):

> In epistemology the contrast between subject and predicate is a contrast between that part of a sentence which serves to identify or designate what is being discussed and that part which serves to describe or characterize the thing so described.

When subject and predicate are so described, the distinction seems very similar to that between topic and comment. In the words of Garver (*ibid.* p. 33) these concepts have to do with: "knowing what is being discussed and understanding what is said about it."

In the following presentation subject—predicate and topic—comment will hence be dealt with as variants of the same general distinction, and our aim is to contrast this distinction with that between free and bound information.

At first sight, the two notions seem very similar. They seem to distinguish between that part of the sentence which has as its primary function to direct the attention of the sender and receiver towards the same state of affairs on the one hand, and that part which is asserted or which provides new information on the other. The fact that context is assumed to influence what will be considered as subject within an utterance (Garver, *ibid.* p. 34) seems further to enhance the similarity between pairs of concepts.

A distinctive feature of the concepts of free and bound information, however, is that they can only be fully applied and understood within a theoretical framework in which word meaning is assumed to be open. This may be clarified by way of an example. If the sentence PROFESSOR ANNE HANSEN IS A REAL WOMAN were uttered in a discussion about professional women, it might be claimed that the segment PROFESSOR ANNE HANSEN provides the free information, while the remaining part of the sentence conveys the bound information. At this rather superficial level of analysis, the distinction thus seems identical to that between subject—predicate (or topic—comment). Such an analysis must be pursued further, however, because identification of free and bound information has to proceed from *what is said* to *what is made known by that which is said.* What is made known by WOMAN is in fact only mediated by a subset of the meaning potentialities of that word. As soon as the name is given, it is taken for granted by both the sender and the receiver that a grown-up person of female sex is being talked about. What is being asserted by WOMAN must consequently reside in semantic potentialities of the word *not already activated* by the use of a female name. The word WOMAN in this particular context might thus suggest that Anne Hansen, although she is a professor, still has many of the personal characteristics traditionally attributed to women, such as, e.g. uncertainty, warmth, etc.

That is, the contextual relevant meaning potentialities of WOMAN may in this case largely have to do with sex-role features and associative and emotive components. *Only the information mediated by such components constitutes in this case the bound information. Generally speaking, what is made known or asserted by specific words must always be understood on the background of what constitutes aspects or parts of the already pre-established shared social world of the participants.*

9.2.2. WHAT IS MESSAGE STRUCTURE?

Message structure may be characterized as a pattern of free and bound information. Both *the dependency relation* and *the nesting aspect* of free and bound information are important in this connection. The concept of message structure thus aims at an explanation of both *the social* and the (intimately related) *temporal aspects of communication.* The nesting aspect of free and bound information is intimately related to the temporal aspect of communication, whereas the dependency relation takes into account its social character. As all aspects of the concepts involved are interrelated, however, we shall in what follows only try to highlight some specific relationships.

We have maintained that *the nesting character* of free and bound information is related to *the temporal aspect* of communication. The nesting characteristic refers to how an intersubjectively and most often only partially shared social world is modified and/or expanded by communication. In the previous section the example of the secretary was used to illustrate the relative character of free and bound information. We tried to show how what was bound information at one stage, at the next stage may be intersubjectively shared and function as free information, for what *then* is made known, and so on.

This nesting of free and bound information is thus compatible with a temporal perspective on communication because it allows us to explore how comprehension evolves over time. No static conception of message transmission follows. On the contrary, the nesting aspect helps us describe in a systematic manner how whatever is intersubjectively given may expand and/or become modified by further communicative activity.

Message structure, however, deals with temporal aspects of communication particularly as related to *the sequence of understanding* or, if both participants are considered, as related to *the sequence in which intersubjectivity is established. It does not refer to the temporal sequence in which information is made available in terms of stimulation or sensory input.* This point will be given more consideration on pp. 175–176.

Rommetveit (1974) explicates what is implied by nesting by an example. A person tries to find out in which one of 16 cells of a square an object is located, and the setting is a simple question-and-answer game. ("Is it in the right half?" "No" "Is it in the upper half of the left half?" "Yes" etc.) By exploring such an example, Rommetveit attempts to show that such a stepwise construction of an intended final state of intersubjectivity—as far as formal aspects is concerned—conforms to "the logic of information theory". We shall not pursue this discussion, however, but only quote a paragraph in which the interrelationship between *sequential structure* and *dependency relations* are clearly pointed out (p. 91):

> What is left of sequential structure in our dialogue when we leave out quantification is namely a particular pattern whereby novel information is nested on to what is already assumed to be the case. Consider, for instance, our initially shared presupposition concerning the square with its 16 cells. It is not only taken for granted as the set of all possible locations of the object, but also tacitly presupposed as the frame of reference whenever proper sense is made of words for direction ("left" *versus* "right") and quantity ("half"). *What is made known at one particular stage is thus not only made part of an expanded shared social reality, but serves at the same time as a prerequisite for making proper sense of what is said at the next stage.* (Last italics mine.)

The prerequisite of convergence upon some information for proper understanding of another part points to the dependency relations within message structure or between free and bound information. This dependency is related to the social character of communication. The aim of a communication act is to expand and/or modify what is intersubjectively shared. As words are open with respect to meaning potentialities, the processing of the bound information has to be dependent upon the free information for proper message transmission. If such constraints on processing did not exist, word meaning processes could develop in whatever direction giving proper message transmission only by chance.

In Chapter 2 we maintained that the sender had more or less control of the sequence of information intake by the receiver. The sender is also, however, ordinarily in control of *what is to be taken for granted.* Understanding *on the premises of the sender* seems thus to imply that one accepts his proposal for free information. Control, moreover, implies power to define a shared social reality. When one of two friends leaving the football-match says to the other: THE OLD MAN IS POOR, referring to a man gathering empty bottles, he suggests that this particular man should be categorized as old. If such a proposal for categorization is accepted by the receiver of the message even though he himself never would have thought of describing the man as OLD, the sender has, in a way, modified his pre-established social reality. (For a discussion of language and power, see Blakar, 1973.)

Such proposals for categorization may be rejected, however. The conversation might thus very well continue as follows:

DO YOU MEAN THE MAN OVER THERE?
YES.
BUT HE IS NOT OLD.

The sender's control is thus by no means absolute, but resides primarily in the fact that he is the one to propose categorizations. His possibilities to affect the receiver's social world may possibly be different, though, when the free information is *tacitly assumed* rather than spelled out. Control is also dependent on particular sequential aspects of communition. In answering a question, for example, my response will thus at least in part be bound to free information inherent in the question.

Message structure appears thus to have a dual character, taking into account both social and temporal aspects of communication. This dual character, moreover, may possibly serve to delimit the range of application of the concept of free information. An explicit discussion of limits seems warranted because free information has at times been used to refer to a too wide range of phenomena (e.g. Rommetveit, 1971, p. 24). The meaning processing of a specific material, or the specific message conveyed by it, is dependent on several factors, but only some of these should properly be called free information. The examples below illustrate factors influencing communication, but which falls outside the range of application of the concept of free information according to our definition.

Rommetveit has on several occasions discussed how the utterance HERE ARE TOO FEW CHAIRS may convey different messages depending on context (see, for example, Rommetveit, 1974, p. 75). The imagined contexts are the following: In one case, the sentence is said by a candidate for a political office who is going to give a political speech and is addressed to the janitor of the building where the meeting is to take place. In such a situation, the janitor will most probably understand the utterance as an order to bring in more chairs. If the same utterance occurs in a telephone call to the wife of the candidate, however, it may probably convey that her husband had gathered a great audience.

In the case of the political candidate and the janitor, we may claim that interpretation of the utterance is determined by reciprocal social roles defining one participant as servant to the other.[1] Such roles may certainly influence message transmission, but are not in themselves either expanded or modified by the utterance. They constitute, in a way, an integral part of a set of relatively stable background factors and should hence *not* be conceived of as free information.

The same seems to be true with another set of factors influencing processing. When I superficially read a newspaper, rapidly looking only at a given heading, I am most probably set for factual information. If precisely the same heading appeared as part of a collage poem, my understanding of it would, one hopes, be different, perhaps in part because I would be much more open towards potential emotive and associative components in the latter case. The I-you axis of communication has changed: It was in the former case defined by *a news reporter*, in the latter case by *a poet* as the sender. This change certainly influences the processing of what I read. The I-you axis, however, is neither expanded nor modified by what goes on in the communication situation, and should hence *not* be conceived of as free information. Thus, the nesting character of free and bound information indicates criteria by which we may distinguish free information (as part of the message structure) from other—in some sense more invariant—prerequisites for communication. Some such other prerequisites are by Rommetveit in part dealt with as "variant premises for intersubjectivity".

9.3. Message structure and experimental results

The concept of message structure has now been discussed at some length within a theoretical frame. The results of a series of experiments referred in this monograph, moreover, testify to its immediate usefulness within experimental research. A main conclusion to be drawn from these experiments is thus that *comprehension and recall performance is enhanced by*

1. Rommetveit (1974) relates the different interpretations to different meta-contracts between sender and receiver in the two cases.

correspondence between message structure and actual sequential presentation of information in real time.

The concepts of *surface-structure* or *deep-structure* cannot explain our pattern of results. The deep-structure of our descriptions remains the same whether the noun is given first or at the end. And a linguistically defined concept of surface-structure is clearly inadequate for assessing what is *made known* by what is said, particularly when such an analysis is expanded to communication in which, e.g. pictorially and verbally provided information is interdependent. The concept of message structure, however, is in itself nevertheless in need of further elaboration, and so is the relationship between message structure and recall performance. Our main experiments resemble traditional verbal learning experiments in which recall is tested in a rather artificial situation. In Experiment C, moreover, the subjects were only asked to reproduce the adjectives of the sentences. This experiment is hence open for the general critique of experiments requiring memory performance only.

One possible interesting expansion of the experiments would be to give different backgrounds or sets of free information to two groups in such a way that free and bound information in what followed would be reversed. If correspondence between temporal sequence and message structure makes for superior recall, it should also be possible to reverse *optimal sequence of presentation* in the two cases.

9.4. Message structure, word openness, and the dimension of time

The importance of *the dimension of time* and the necessity of a conception of *word meaning as open and dynamic* were emphasized in the theoretical framework of Part I. In the experimental part, temporal aspects were attended to both in connection with *sequence of presentation* of words as well as in our analysis of *the processing of the material*. Via a route including several excursions into theories of impression formation and memory, we then ended up with the general concept of message structure as a particular promising avenue to further insight.

One important question remains to be answered, however. To what extent are our initial notions of word meaning as open and considerations bearing upon the dimension of time incorporated in the concept of message structure? The answer to this general question has already been suggested in our discussion of free and bound information and message structure. Because of the importance of this issue, however, some additional reflections seem warranted.

The openness of word meaning and the dependency aspect of message structure are closely related: Once we realize that word meaning changes depending upon context, we also have to specify *which factors influence processing*. And the notion of message structure with its basis in the dependency relation between free and bound information aims at explication of both *patterns* and *direction* of influence. It thus brings us far beyond the rather vague claim that "word meaning is open and influenced by context". (For a discussion of another relevant concept, contract, see Blakar, 1975. For a more general presentation, see Rommetveit, 1974.)

The dimension of time is of central significance in the nesting aspect of message structure. In our initial discussion of temporal aspects of oral language, we merely emphasized the obvious fact that all events—also language events—take place in real time and have therefore a temporal dimension. The dimension of time was thus conceived in a rather concrete manner, and the interest in sequence problems and in the process of understanding both reflected this concrete conception.

Nesting of bound to free information has to do with temporality in an indirect and much more abstract sense. This nesting is neither directly related to strategy of processing nor to sequence of presentation. The message structure of A SECRETARY WHO IS SEVERE, COOL, EXTRAORDINARY, BEAUTIFUL, PLEASANT is identical to that of A SEVERE, COOL, EXTRAORDINARY, BEAUTIFUL, PLEASANT SECRETARY in spite of different sequences of words and—most probably—also different strategies of processing.

The dimension of time concretely understood is thus not as such incorporated into the concept of message structure. But—and this is important—an explication of message structure seems to be a prerequisite if we want to explore psychological consequences of actual sequences of information. In order to gain insight into the ways in which order of presentation affects decoding and comprehension, it is thus essential to know whether or not there is correspondence between message structure and temporal order.

The concept of message structure seems thus a useful concept when openness of word meaning and the dimension of time are conceived as basic aspects of language. From one perspective, it represents an attempt to conceptualize factors influencing the meaning processing. From

176   DECODING ORAL LANGUAGE

another perspective, the concept is useful because an analysis of message structure seems to be revealing when the time dimension and the possible effect of different sequences come in focus of attention.

Inherent in the concept of message structure is also the need for an analysis of *what already constitutes the shared social world of the participants* in an act of communication. This must be determined before the consequences of any specific sequence of information can be assessed. Thus, the consequences of a construction such as A SEVERE, COOL, EXTRAORDINARY, BEAUTIFUL, PLEASANT SECRETARY will clearly be different from those observed in our experiments if it were already known, either by previous verbally mediated information or by inference, that a secretary is being talked about. When language is to be understood with due attention towards the dimension of time, we have thus simultaneously to take into account *the concrete sequencing of elements and the more abstract sequential structure of the expansion and/or modification of what is intersubjectively shared.*

9.5. Some further reflections related to the concept of message structure

The relationship between *process* and *structure* has been commented upon on several occasions, and our confessed primary interest has been processing. But what, then, about the concept of message structure? Its very name implies reference to some structure and hence—possibly—to a-temporal entities.

The a-temporality of deep-structure and surface-structure does not pertain to message structure, however. Message structure has a temporal aspect by virtue of its inherent, abstract sequential structure. It has, even though in itself not a true process-concept, immediate implications for processing. It has implications for patterns of influence or dependency among segments of information and—in combination with information of actual sequences of information—implications for memory processes as well.

The final issue to be explored may perhaps best be introduced via some unresolved problems in two experiments on the relationship between what is seen and what is heard (Rommetveit *et al.*, 1971; Blakar and Rommetveit, 1975). The problems concern the possibility *that different individuals may organize the very same externally provided information differently, and in such ways that different message structures are generated.*

A general outline of the experiment by Rommetveit *et al.* was given on pp. 143–144, and the Blakar and Rommetveit study represents essentially a modified and expanded version of the former. The stimulus material consisted in both experiments of combinations of pictures and spoken sentences. Although the former were described as ready signals for the sentences by the experimenter, they clearly influenced the processing of the subsequent sentence. This conclusion is supported by the fact that the recall performance of the subjects was different depending on the relationship between the visual information and the sentence heard. When the figures represented reasonable contexts for the subsequent sentences the recall performance was better than when the figures were geometrical drawings unrelated to the sentences.

In the experiment by Rommetveit *et al.* a facilitating effect of relevant picture contexts upon recall of utterances was obtained only for a particular subset of the sentences used in the experiment, however. In these cases, the combination of picture and utterance was such that the pictorially provided context induced a constraint upon possible interpretations of the subsequent utterance. The picture may hence in these cases be said to provide *free information* relative to what is conveyed by the utterance. For the remaining subset of sentences, on the other hand, final interpretation of picture seemed to be dependent on what would be made known by the utterance to follow. The sentence thus served to convey free information. Relevant picture contexts thus facilitated recall only in cases of *correspondence between message structure and temporal order*. So far, therefore, the results are in perfect correspondence with those from our main experiments.

This interpretation appears more problematic, however, once the results from the Blakar and Rommetveit study are taken into consideration as well. In the latter study, the facilitating effect of a relevant picture context was again displayed, *but no significant effect of the different types of relevant picture—utterance combination was observed.*

Blakar and Rommetveit argue that the difference in results may be due to the different groups of subjects participating in the two studies. In the Rommetveit *et al.* study, the subjects were soldiers with on the average only one-and-a-half years of additional education beyond elementary school. In the Blakar and Rommetveit study, on the other hand, university students served as subjects. These two groups differ widely with respect to intellectual background and training, and it is thus possible that they related the picture and the subsequent sentence in different ways. Differences with respect to cognitive capacity might hence explain why one subset of the pictures facilitated recall only when students served as subjects. Blakar and Rommetveit (p. 26) suggest more specifically, that the students in these cases may have "reorganized what was jointly made known by picture and utterance AS A CAUSAL CONNECTION" and that such an organization gives correspondence between message structure and temporal order also for these items.

Let us consider, more closely, the suggestion that picture and sentence may be *related* in different ways by the two subject groups. It is also possible that the students do relate the two different components of information, but that these remain unrelated for the soldiers. If so, the information provided by picture and sentence will not be incorporated into the same message. Consequently, it seems, in that case, meaningless to talk about cases of noncorrespondence between message structure and temporal order.

These additional comments are warranted because the latter study has been referred to as providing evidence in support of the superiority of pre-position of free information. (Rommetveit, 1972; Blakar and Rommetveit, *ibid.*) If information from picture and utterance remains unrelated in the study by Rommetveit *et al.*, however, resemblance to our main experiment may be questioned.

The main point to be made in connection with the studies by Rommetveit *et al.* and by Blakar and Rommetveit at this stage, however, has to do with the possibility that different individuals may relate the same information in different ways so that qualitatively different message structures emerge. This seems to remain true whether the soldiers actually managed to relate pictures and sentences as components of a unitary message or not. In both cases would their message structure for one half of the items differ from that of the students. This, in turn, implies a serious complication in any intuitively based assessment of message structure.

These problems lead us back to our dual *social* and *individual* perspective on communication. If an individual does not have the cognitive capacity to relate potentially related different components of information, these cannot become part of some cognitive entity. If one component is totally forgotten when a second one is presented, moreover, these components of information cannot be incorporated into the same message structure.

The concept of message structure as explicated so far thus leaves us with a number of residual problems, only some of which have been touched upon here. Further explorations are therefore required. Such further explorations are also warranted in view of the promising features of the concept. We have in our previous discussion tried to show how it may serve to bring together results from different experiments into a unitary exploratory framework, a framework by which both social and temporal aspects of communication can be explored jointly and in a systematic manner.

10

Final Comments

In the present work relatively unequivocal experimental evidence has been established in support of the importance of temporal sequence for impression formation and recall. Such results suggest that a systematic exploration of sequence problems might be revealing also within other areas, and we want to conclude this monograph with some reflections on the possibility of adopting the present theoretical approach in other contexts as well. Instead of attempting a comprehensive survey of potential novel areas, however, we shall only comment briefly upon some selected examples.

Issues having to do with temporal sequence are probably of particular importance in diagnosis and communication with persons with a marginal linguistic competence. The difference between pre-position versus post-position of free information may thus indeed mark the difference between *being able* versus *not being able to understand* for young children, mentally retarded and other categories of people with specific language problems. Consider, for instance, the task of testing a mentally retarded child. If the instruction is carefully constructed with perfect correspondence between word order and message structure, the child may possibly succeed. If not, a failure may result. And this may be the case even if the task as such involves purely motor performance.

Such considerations may at present appear speculative. But the results already at hand seem to indicate that careful attention should be paid to the sequencing of information in such situations. Examples reported by Luria (1966) from the investigation of the understanding of logical grammatical structures by different groups of aphasic patients, moreover, point in the same direction.

Consider, for instance, the following task: Three objects are placed in front of the patient (e.g. a pencil, a comb and a key). The patient is told: POINT WITH THE COMB TOWARD THE PENCIL and then: POINT TO THE PENCIL WITH THE COMB. Some aphasic patients tend to *manage* the task when given the first instruction, but fail to do so when receiving the second instruction (*ibid.* p. 386). *That is, they manage the task if there is correspondence between word order and the sequence of actions to be performed, but fail in cases of non-correspondence.* In the latter cases, they still continue to act according to the order in which the words were presented, pointing *with* the pencil *to* the comb.

In the examples given by Luria, correspondence/non-correspondence concerns *word order* and *action*. In the present work, on the other hand, word order has been explored as related to sequence of understanding. But comprehension appears to be an essential link between a verbal instruction and performance of the act described by that instruction as well. And non-correspondence implies in both cases an element of postponement, of keeping something in mind in anticipation of further information for some short time.

In view of the discussion above, serious concern with individual differences appears to be a prerequisite for a more broad understanding of sequence problems. We have discussed instances in which apparently some linguistically determined request for postponement made the subjects unable to perform a task. We may now broaden our perspective and explore more generally, how *relative ease of pre-position versus post-position of free information* may relate to other psychologically important individual differences. And we shall then, first of all, comment briefly upon developmental differences of possible relevance.

Two factors seem then to be of particular importance. First, *memory span* increases as children grow older (see, for example, the norms given for Auditory Sequential Memory in the "Examiner's Manual of Illinois Test of Psycholinguistic Abilities", Kirk, McCarthy and Kirk, 1968). Since the difference between pre-position and post-position of free information implies differential strain on memory, it could be expected that children should have relatively greater problems than the grown-up in cases of post-position of free information.

A second factor of importance has to do with aquisition of semantic competence and the fact that word meaning changes as children grow older. Asch and Nerlove (1967) explored how the understanding of so-called double function terms changes during the years from three to twelve. Double function terms are adjectives that can be used to describe both physical and psychological data (e.g. adjectives such as HARD, COLD, SWEET), and many of the adjectives in our descriptions would thus fall within this class.

Asch and Nerlove report that such adjectives were understood mainly with reference to their *object characteristic* by the two youngest groups of children, the three- to four-year-old group and the five- to six-year-old group. Thus, in the few instances in which the terms were used to describe persons, they were predominantly used to refer to physical characteristics. If asked to explain how they knew that a person had a given quality, replies like the following would be given:

SANTA CLAUS IS WARM BECAUSE HE HAS A LONG BEARD, DADDY AND MOMMY ARE DEEP BECAUSE THEY LOOK BIG

This is in contrast to the older groups which showed a more adequate understanding of the psychological sense of the terms, explaining for example that HARD PEOPLE ARE TOUGH AND SOLDIERLIKE.

The small child's relatively "closed" and sensory bound interpretations of double function terms may influence his decoding in that it relieves him from the adults' commitment to postpone final decoding. Semantic competence may hence also possibly influence the relative ease of pre-position versus post-position of free information. Further experimental studies are required, however, for a better understanding of developmental changes with respect to mastery of post-position of free information.

So far, our final comments have been restricted to problems of language and communication. Our general approach to these issues, however, may prove of value within other areas as well. And while sequence is important to every one of us, it is probably of particular importance to one specific group of people—*the blind*. Our arguments for the general importance of the dimension of time, should not be taken to imply *equal importance* within all areas. More specifically, the significance of sequence problems seems to vary with modality, with vision as the most "spatial" of our senses.

As a consequence of loss of vision, the blind person has to gain information through other senses, particularly the tactile-kinesthetic and the auditory senses, each of which is to a much greater extent characterized by sequential intake of information. Although it takes some short time to experience a room by vision, it certainly requires much more time if the same room is to be experienced via touch and movements. This means, generally, that the blind are forced to *integrate information taken in over time* to a greater extent than people with intact vision. Different sequences of information intake thus become of particular importance.

This perspective is important when we compare performances: If we present a task where all the necessary information is simultaneously present (for example, by objects in space) to a blind person and a person with normal vision, the task actually differs between the two. Because the blind person has to experience different parts of the entire information sequentially, temporal integration becomes of much greater importance for him.

The considerations above have one implicit presupposition—the necessity to integrate. If information could simply be retained in its sequential form, the blind person's difficulties would be greatly reduced. This seems impossible in many cases, however. Solution of most tasks requires that relevant components of information have to be related and compared in different ways. This means that separate parts or fragments of information have to be simultaneously present in one way or another. If they are not present more or less directly to the senses, they have to be present in memory.

Integration is thus essential in many spheres of our problem solving and general orientation in life. Thus, at least part of the conception of what a house is, develops from sensory experiences. If one is blind, these sensory experiences may be accumulated by moving around the house, by moving within the rooms, by touching the floor, the walls and so on. The resultant different pieces of sensory information have to be organized in one way or another, however, in order to become part of a unitary conception of house. The necessity to organize them into a—in some sense—*simultaneous* experience is very cogently brought to our attention in an answer from a young blind man. When asked how he imagined the room in which he lived, he answered that *he pretended to be all over the room at once.*

In addition to the more general relevance of sequence problems within the world of the blind, it seems also possible to relate their experiences more specifically to what happens in situations with post-position of free information. The blind person often has to touch something without knowing what it is, and his final interpretation of sensations has then to be postponed until he knows *what* he explores. His problem is thus formally similar to the postponement of final decoding of adjectives in

Noun-end descriptions: Until the noun is given, final interpretation of
the adjectives have to remain open. If a word—or a particular sensation
—is interpreted prematurely, moreover, the interpretation may be
wrong, and reinterpretation is then required at a later stage.

Carling (1962) has in one of his novels given a very vivid description
of a blind man's encounter with a sculpture. His description may actually serve as an illustration of postponement of free information and
what may happen in cases of misinterpretation. The blind man has
been touching the sculpture for some time, believing that it is a sculpture of a man, a monk. Carling then corrects him, however, and tells
him that he is touching a sculpture of Camilla Collett, a woman strongly
engaged in the emancipation of women. The reaction of the blind man
to this information is described by Carling as follows (*ibid.* p. 22):

> It seemed to me that his face expressed surprise and disappointment, and
> I could see how his internal picture of the strict monk, a picture created
> by his experience, by his fantasy, was broken by what I had told him. His
> hands glided testingly over the body for still some time, but it appeared as
> if the touching could no longer tell him anything. (Translation mine.)

In this specific case, a reinterpretation would require so much novel
engagement that the blind person did not even venture to try.

In this brief excursion into the problems of the blind, we have only
touched upon some of their sequence problems. We have tried to show,
however, how some of the central theoretical notions in the present
monograph may be brought to bear upon problems of immediate
practical importance within a challenging area of theoretical and
applied research. This latter area, however, deserves a much more
penetrating analysis than has been attempted here.

APPENDICES

Appendix A

Redundancy of the Descriptions

Sixteen students, nine male and seven female, served as subjects. These students came from the same student population as those serving in the main experiments.

The subjects were given small booklets in which the six different combinations of adjectives used in Experiments I and II were written, one set of adjectives on each page, and asked to write down the first thing, happening or person these combinations made them think of. The adjective order was varied between A_1–A_5 and A_5–A_1. The results from all 16 subjects were pooled together, however, partly because lack of control of sequence of information intake for written presentations, and partly because the small number of subjects participating.

The results are presented in qualitative form. How often the subjects respond to a particular combination of adjectives with a noun identical to or rather similar to the noun actually used in the experiment, is of

Nouns used in the experiment	The nouns from the redundancy task which seem similar to those from the experiments	Comments
1. SECRETARY	WOMAN (3), A SPECIAL SORT OF WOMEN, TEACHER (2), A GIRL WHO FASCINATES ME, LADY, FEMALE BOSS, FEMALE PSYCHOLOGIST	Ten of the 16 subjects think of women. One person mentions MAN which make 11 subjects who mention persons. Some of the other nouns have to do with the climate, e.g. WEATHER, SUMMER

Nouns used in the experiment	The nouns from the redundancy task which seem similar to those from the experiments	Comments
2. CHAIR	OLD SOFA	Every other noun is very 'far from' CHAIR. The variability between the nouns is relatively great although five subjects respond with words referring in one way or another to a person. Other examples are: CAT, ELEPHANT, TRUNK, SWAMP
3. MOVIE		None of the words are similar to MOVIE. EXAMINATION is reported four times and is the most frequent response. Seven subjects answer with nouns referring to persons in one way or another. Other examples are: SOCIETY, DEAD ANIMALS
4. ACTRESS	WOMAN, MOST OF THE WOMEN, CABARET DANCER, LIZ TAYLOR	Four subjects respond with nouns similar to ACTRESS, two of these appear to be very much similar. One subject reports BOY. This means that five subjects think of persons. Other examples are: OCEAN, LOVE, CAT
5. FARMER	OLD MAN (2), SOCRATES, MEN	Four subjects give answers somewhat similar to FARMER. Rather many subjects respond with nouns like GRAND-MOTHER, OLD WOMAN. Eleven subjects think of persons. Other examples are: FOREST, HOUSE
6. BOOK		The answer given which appear to be most closely related to BOOK, is DREAM. Every other noun seems to be very different in meaning. Four subjects report BEAR. Two subjects think of persons. Other examples are: HOUSE, TICKET

primary interest. The numbers in the overview refer to how many subjects gave a particular answer.

This overview testifies to one conclusion. The similarity between the nouns used in the descriptions of the experiment and the nouns reported by the subjects in the redundancy task is much more prominent in relation to descriptions referring to persons (SECRETARY, ACTRESS, FARMER) than in relation to the other nouns (CHAIR, MOVIE, BOOK). In the latter group, almost none of the nouns reported is similar in meaning to the noun of the description.

Appendix B

Natural Order of Adjectives

The sequence of adjectives within a description was decided by a procedure by which it was tried to reach what might be called the "natural order" of these specific adjectives when used to characterize the given noun.

The "frames" of the six descriptions, that is the descriptions with the adjective part left open, were given in written form to 14 subjects (students). Seven subjects were given the frames from Noun-first description, and seven subjects were given the frames from Noun-end descriptions. The five adjectives from each description were also given, presented in alphabetic order. The task of the subjects was only to order the adjectives as natural as possible when they were used to describe the given noun.

The sequence chosen as the most natural varied between subjects, and the adjectives were seldom arranged in identical order by two subjects. In order to summarize the results, two sets of six matrices were used. The information taken out to form these matrices was only how often the different adjectives followed each of the other. The matrices for CHAIR, called first and second matrix of CHAIR, are given below as an example.

The first matrix of CHAIR is to be understood in the following way: GREY was ordered *after* DREARY by four subjects, SOFT was given this position by 1 subject and so on. In addition to the information within the cells, the marginal numbers are also informative in that they contain information about how many times a specific adjective was given in first and last position. When different adjectives have followed DREARY nine times, it means that in the rest of the cases (5) no adjective followed DREARY, that is, it was given in last position. Similarly,

DREARY followed other adjectives 12 times, which means that this word has not followed any adjective in two cases, that is, it was given in first position.

The information in the first matrix has primarily been used to decide which word should be given in first position. The adjective most often given in this position by the subjects has been chosen. For CHAIR, this is SOFT.

First matrix of CHAIR

	DREARY	GREY	SOFT	TALL	UGLY	
DREARY		4	1	2	2	9
GREY	7		1	2	4	14
SOFT	2	3		5	2	12
TALL	0	5	4		4	13
UGLY	3	2	2	1		8
	12	14	8	10	12	

Second matrix of CHAIR

	DREARY	GREY	SOFT	TALL	UGLY
DREARY		11	3	2	5
GREY			4	7	6
SOFT				9	4
TALL					5
UGLY					

To decide on the sequence of the other adjectives, the second matrix of CHAIR has been used. Here it is only shown how many times all different pairs of words have occurred independent of the sequence within these pairs.

In order to understand how the information concretely is used, we may describe how the order of the adjectives following SOFT has been decided. The second matrix reveals that TALL is the adjective that most frequently occurred in close connection with SOFT. It is therefore given second position. GREY is more often given together with TALL than any of the remaining adjectives and is thus given third position and so on.

A procedure similar to the one here described in some detail for CHAIR was used to order adjectives within each description.

Appendix C

The Evaluation of Adjectives and Nouns

The evaluation of adjectives and nouns was done rather informally, by asking eight colleagues to serve as co-judges.

Fifty-one words were to be rated on a seven-point evaluative scale similar to the one used in the impression formation part of Experiments I and II. The list of 51 words included every adjective from the experimental descriptions presented with its appropriate noun as context word in the following way: (FARMER) ATTRACTIVE. The subjects were asked to rate how positive or negative they judged the adjective to be when it was used to characterize this special noun. In addition to the 30 adjectives presented with context words, the six experimental nouns, and the 15 adjectives used in the examples in the instruction were included in the list. The last 15 adjectives were presented without any context word.

The sequence in which the words were presented was random, constrained, however, in the following way: There should always be at least three words between two adjectives from the same set. There should never be two nouns or two adjectives without context words following each other.

The results for the words in the descriptions are given below by just writing down the average ratings above the descriptions. The descriptions are given in Norwegian because it seems meaningless to imply that the English adjectives suggested as translations should receive the same evaluation.

We may first notice that every noun used in the descriptions receives a value between 4 and 5 which means that they all fall within the range from medium to good.

4·3	5·6	5·3	4·5	3·4	3·3
SEKRETÆR	BEHAGELIG	SKJØNN	UVANLIG	KJØLIG	STRENG
(SECRETARY)					

4·1	5·1	3·4	3·3	2·4	2·0
STOL	MYK	HØY	GRÅ	TRIST	STYGG
(CHAIR)					

4·8	5·5	5·4	5·0	2·4	2·4
FILM	BETYDNINGSFULL	KREVENDE	MERKELIG	VEMMELIG	ØDELAGT
(MOVIE)					

4·5	5·3	6·0	3·9	4·4	2·8
SKUESPILLERINNE	MANGFOLDIG	SPENNENDE	VAKKER	REN	LUMSK
(ACTRESS)					

4·6	5·6	5·5	4·0	4·4	4·5
BONDE	VENNLIG	TILTREKKENDE	MØRK	GAMMEL	TETT
(FARMER)					

5·0	3·9	3·9	3·5	1·8	2·5
BOK	STOR	BRUN	DYSTER	FANTASILØS	ROTETE
(BOOK)					

The sequence of adjectives within a description is surprisingly regular. For SEKRETÆR, STOL, FILM (SECRETARY, CHAIR, MOVIE) the sequence fits exactly what might be called a descending order. The most positive adjectives occupy the first positions, followed by the words with second highest ratings and so on. For SKUESPILLERINNE, BONDE, BOK (ACTRESS, FARMER, BOOK) the order is not so regular, still showing, however, a tendency toward the same descending order.

Appendix D Tables

Table D1

Average number of adjectives recalled to each noun
Experiment I

| Description | Noun-first | | | Noun-end | | | Average description |
	Condition I A_1–A_5	Condition II A_5–A_1	Average Noun-first	Condition III A_1–A_5	Condition IV A_5–A_1	Average Noun-end	
ACTRESS	1·8	1·8	1·8	0·8	0·6	0·7	1·2
MOVIE	1·3	0·8	1·0	0·5	0·7	0·6	0·8
FARMER	2·5	2·7	2·6	0·9	1·6	1·3	1·9
CHAIR	3·1	2·1	2·6	1·2	1·5	1·4	2·0
BOOK	2·0	2·5	2·2	0·8	1·3	1·1	1·6
SECRETARY	1·2	1·1	1·1	0·7	0·9	0·8	0·9
Average pr. person	11·7	10·9	11·3	4·8	6·5	5·7	8·5

Table D2

Average number of adjectives recalled to each noun
Experiment II

| Description | Noun-first | | | Noun-end | | | Average description |
	Condition I_N A_1–A_5	Condition II_N A_5–A_1	Average Noun-first	Condition III_N A_1–A_5	Condition IV_N A_5–A_1	Average Noun-end	
ACTRESS	1·2	1·4	1·3	0·8	0·8	0·8	1·0
MOVIE	0·6	0·3	0·4	0·5	0·5	0·5	0·5
FARMER	1·8	2·4	2·1	1·0	1·4	1·2	1·6
CHAIR	2·6	2·7	2·6	1·2	1·6	1·4	2·0
BOOK	1·2	1·6	1·4	0·8	0·9	0·8	1·1
SECRETARY	1·0	1·0	1·0	0·8	0·6	0·7	0·8
Average pr. person	8·3	9·2	8·7	5·0	5·8	5·4	7·0

Table D3

Positional recall of adjectives
Experiment I

| Position | Noun-first | | | Noun-end | | | Average position |
	Condition I A_1–A_5	Condition II A_5–A_1	Average Noun-first	Condition III A_1–A_5	Condition IV A_5–A_1	Average Noun-end	
1	3·1	2·2	2·6	0·4	0·8	0·6	1·6
2	2·8	1·1	2·0	1·1	0·5	0·8	1·4
3	2·6	2·2	2·4	1·2	1·0	1·1	1·7
4	1·6	3·1	2·3	0·7	2·1	1·4	1·9
5	1·7	2·4	2·0	1·5	2·3	1·9	1·9
Average pr. person	11·7	10·9	11·3	4·8	6·5	5·7	8·5

Table D4

Positional recall of adjectives
Experiment II

| Position | Noun-first | | | Noun-end | | | Average position |
	Condition I_N A_1–A_5	Condition II_N A_5–A_1	Average Noun-first	Condition III_N A_1–A_5	Condition IV_N A_1–A_5	Average Noun-end	
1	1·9	1·7	1·8	0·8	0·7	0·7	1·3
2	2·1	0·7	1·4	1·6	0·5	1·0	1·2
3	1·8	1·8	1·8	1·0	1·5	1·2	1·5
4	1·2	2·9	2·0	0·2	1·5	0·9	1·4
5	1·4	2·3	1·8	1·5	1·6	1·6	1·7
Average pr. person	8·3	9·2	8·7	5·0	5·8	5·4	7·0

Table D5

Positional recall of adjectives recalled in response to correct and incorrect noun
Experiment I

Position	Noun-first Condi-tion I A_1–A_5	Condi-tion II A_5–A_1	Aver-age Noun-first	Noun-end Condi-tion III A_1–A_5	Condi-tion IV A_5–A_1	Aver-age Noun-end	Aver-age position
1	3·1	2·4	2·8	0·7	1·3	1·0	1·9
2	3·1	1·3	2·2	2·2	1·0	1·6	1·9
3	2·9	2·7	2·8	1·9	1·9	1·9	2·3
4	2·0	3·5	2·8	1·4	2·4	1·9	2·3
5	2·0	2·5	2·2	1·9	2·5	2·2	2·2
Average pr. person	13·0	12·3	12·7	8·0	9·1	8·5	10·6

Table D6

Positional recall of adjectives recalled in response to correct and incorrect noun
Experiment II

Position	Noun-first Condi-tion I_N A_1–A_5	Condi-tion II_N A_5–A_1	Aver-age Noun-first	Noun-end Condi-tion III_N A_1–A_5	Condi-tion IV_N A_5–A_1	Aver-age Noun-end	Aver-age position
1	2·1	1·8	1·9	1·0	1·1	1·0	1·5
2	2·3	1·1	1·7	2·4	0·8	1·6	1·6
3	2·0	2·3	2·1	1·4	2·1	1·7	1·9
4	1·6	3·2	2·4	0·9	2·1	1·5	1·9
5	1·7	2·5	2·1	1·7	1·8	1·7	1·9
Average pr. person	9·6	10·7	10·1	7·2	7·8	7·5	8·8

Table D7

Positional recall of words recalled in response to first adjective as prompt word
Experiment II

Position	Noun-first Condition I_A A_1–A_5	Condition II_A A_5–A_1	Average Noun-first	Noun-end Condition III_A A_1–A_5	Condition IV_A A_5–A_1	Average Noun-end	Average position
Noun	3·8	2·8	3·3				
2	1·8	0·5	1·1	0·6	0·3	0·4	0·8
3	1·5	0·8	1·1	0·2	0·6	0·4	0·8
4	1·0	1·4	1·2	0·1	0·3	0·2	0·7
5	1·2	0·9	1·0	0·2	0·3	0·2	0·6
Noun				1·1	0·8	0·9	
Average pr. person	9·1	6·2	7·7	2·1	2·2	2·1	

References

Allport, F. H. (1962). "Theories of Perception and the Concept of Structure." John Wiley, New York.

Anderson, N. H. (1965). Primacy effects in personality impression formation using a generalized order effect paradigm. *Journal of Personality and Social Psychology*, 2, 1–9.

Anderson, N. H. (1968). Application of a linear-serial model to a personality-impression task using serial presentation. *Journal of Personality and Social Psychology*, 10, 354–362.

Anderson, N. H. and Barrios, A. A. (1961). Primacy effects in personality impression formation. *Journal of Abnormal and Social Psychology*, 63, 346–350.

Anderson, N. H. and Hubert, S. (1963). Effects of concomitant verbal recall on order effects on personality impression formation. *Journal of Verbal Learning and Verbal Behavior*, 2, 379–391.

Anderson, N. H. and Norman, A. (1964). Order effects in impression formation in four classes of stimuli. *Journal of Abnormal and Social Psychology*, 69, 467–471.

Asch, S. E. (1946). Forming impression of personality. *Journal of Abnormal and Social Psychology*, 41, 258–290.

Asch, S. E. and Nerlove, H. (1967). The development of double function terms in children: An exploratory investigation. *In* "The Psychology of Language, Thought, and Instruction. Readings" (J. P. De Cecco, ed.). pp. 283–290. Holt, Rinehart and Winston, New York.

Atkinson, R. C. and Shiffrin, R. M. (1968). Human memory: A proposed system and its control processes. *In* "The Psychology of Learning and Motivation". (K. W. Spence and J. T. Spence, eds). Vol. 2, pp. 89–195. Academic Press, New York.

Baddeley, A. D. (1970). Estimating the short-term component in free-recall. *British Journal of Psychology*, 61, 13–15.

Baddeley, A. D. and Dale, H. C. A. (1966). The effect of semantic similarity on retroactive interference in long- and short-term memory. *Journal of Verbal Learning and Verbal Behavior*, 5, 417–420.

Bakker, D. J. (1972). "Temporal Order in Disturbed Reading". Rotterdam University Press, Rotterdam.

Barrett, W. (1962). Introduction (to phenomenology and existentialism). *In* "Philosophy in the Twentieth Century. An Anthology". (W. Barrett and H. D. Aiken, eds) Vol. 3, pp. 125–169. Random House, New York.

Bergson, H. (1962). Time in the history of Western Philosophy. *In* "Philosophy in the Twentieth Century. An Anthology (W. Barret and H. D. Aiken, eds) Vol. 3, pp. 331–363. Random House, New York.

Blakar, R. M. (1970). Konteksteffektar i språkleg kommunikasjon. Unpublished thesis, Institute of Psychology, University of Oslo.

Blakar, R. M. (1973). "Språk er Makt". Pax Forlag A/S, Oslo.

Blakar, R. M. (1975). Human communication—an ever changing contract embedded in social contexts. Mimeo. Institute of Psychology, University of Oslo.

Blakar, R. M. and Rommetveit, R. (1975). Utterances in vacuo and in contexts: An experimental and theoretical exploration of some interrlationships between what is heard and what is seen or imagined. *Linguistics*, **153**, 5–32.

Blumenthal, A. L. (1967). Prompted recall of sentences. *Journal of Verbal Learning and Verbal Behavior*, **6**, 203–206.

Blumenthal, A. L. and Boakes, R. (1967). Prompted recall of sentences. *Journal of Verbal Learning and Verbal Behavior*, **6**, 674–676.

Bolinger, D. L. (1963). The uniqueness of the word. *Lingua*, **12**, 113–136.

Boring, E. G. (1957). "A History of Experimental Psychology". Second edition. Appleton-Century-Crofts, New York.

Bransford, I. D. and Johnson, M. K. (1973). Considerations of some problems of comprehension. *In* "Visual Information Processing". (W. G. Chase, ed) pp. 383–438, Academic Press, New York.

Briscoe, M. E., Woodyard, H. D. and Shaw, M. E. (1967). Personality impression change as a function of the favorableness of first impressions. *Journal of Personality*, **35**, 343–357.

Broen, P. A. (1972). "The Verbal Environment of the Language-Learning Child". ASHA Monographs, no 17. American Speech and Hearing Association, Washington.

Brown, R. (1958). "Words and Things". The Free Press, Glencoe, Illinois.

Brown, R. (1965). "Social Psychology" 5.print. The Free Press, New York. Collier-MacMillan Limited, London.

Carling, F. (1962). "Blind Verden". Gyldendal Norsk Forlag.

Chomsky, N. (1957). "Syntactic Structures". Mouton, The Hague.

Chomsky, N. (1965). "Aspects of the Theory of Syntax". The M.I.T. Press, Cambridge, Mass.

Chomsky, N. (1968). "Language and Mind". Harcourt, Brace and World, New York.

Chomsky, N. (1973). "Studies on Semantics in Generative Grammar". Mouton, The Hague.

Collaizzi, P. F. (1971). The phenomenology of Merleau-Ponty and the serial position effect. *Journal of Phenomenological Psychology*, **2**, 115–123.

Craik, F. I. M. (1973). A "levels of analysis" view of memory. *In* "Communication and Affect. Language and Thought". (P. Pliner, L. Krames and T. Alloway, eds) pp. 45–65. Academic Press, New York.

Craik, F. I. M. and Lockhart, R. S. (1972). Levels of processing: A framework for memory research. *Journal of Verbal Learning and Verbal Behavior*, **11**, 671–684.

Crowder, R. G. (1969). Behavioral strategies in immediate memory. *Journal of Verbal Learning and Verbal Behavior*, **8**, 524–528.

Deese, J and Kaufman, R. A. (1957). Serial effects in recall of unorganized and sequentially organized verbal material. *Journal of Experimental Psychology*, **54**, 180–187.

Efron, R. (1963). Temporal perception, aphasia and déjà vu. *Brain*, **86**, 406–424.

Fillenbaum, S. (1970). The use of memorial techniques to assess syntactic structures. *Psychological Bulletin*, **73**, 231–237.

Fillenbaum, S. (1971). Psycholinguistics. *Annual Review of Psychology*, **22**, 251–308.

Fillenbaum, S. (1973). "Syntactic Factors in Memory?" Mouton, The Hague.

Fillmore, C. J. (1972). Subjects, speakers and roles. *In* "Semantics of Natural Language" (D. Davidson and G. Harman, eds). pp. 1–24, D. Reidel Publishing Company, Dordrecht, Holland.

Fodor, J. A. and Bever, T. G. (1965). The psychological reality of linguistic segments. *Journal of Verbal Learning and Verbal Behavior*, **4**, 414–420.

Garrett, M., Bever, T. G. and Fodor, J. A. (1966). The active use of grammar in speech perception. *Perception and Psychophysics*, **1**, 30–32.

Garver, N. (1967). Subject and predicate. *In* "The Encyclopedia of Philosophy" (P. Edwards ed.) Vol. 8, pp. 33–36. The MacMillan Company and The Free Press, New York. Collier-MacMillan Limited, London.

Glanzer, M. (1972). Storage mechanisms in recall. *In* "The Psychology of Learning and Motivation". (G. H. Bower, ed.) Vol. 5, pp. 129–193. Academic Press, New York.

Glanzer, M. and Cunitz, A. R. (1966). Two storage mechanisms in free recall. *Journal of Verbal Learning and Verbal Behavior*, **5**, 351–360.

Glass, G. V. and Stanley, J. C. (1970). "Statistical Methods in Education and Psychology". Prentice-Hall, Englewood Cliffs, New Jersey.

Goldman-Eisler, F. (1968). "Psycholinguistics: Experiments in Spontaneous Speech". Academic Press, London.

Goodglass, H., Gleason, J. and Hyde, M. (1970). Some dimensions of auditory language comprehension in aphasia. *Journal of Speech and Hearing Research*, **13**, 595–606.

Goodglass, H. and Kaplan, E. (1972). "The Assessment of Aphasia and Related Disorders". Lea and Febiger, Philadelphia.

Helstrup, T. (1973). "Kognitive Prosesser i Kort-tids Hukommelse". Institute of Psychology, University of Bergen.

Herriot, P. (1974). "Attributes of Memory". Methuen, London.

Hockett, C. F. (1963). The problem of universals in language. *In* "Universals of Language". (J. H. Greenberg, ed.) pp. 1–22. The M.I.T. Press, Cambridge, Mass.

Hovland, C. J. (Ed.) (1966). "The Order of Presentation in Persuasion". Yale University Print, New Haven and London, 3.print.

Jakobson, R. (1971). Two aspects of language and two types of aphasic disturbances. *In* "Fundamentals of Language". (R. Jakobson and M. Halle) Second edition, Mouton, The Hague.

Jaspars, J. (1966). "On Social Perception". Proefschrift ter verkrijging van de graad van Doctor in de Sociale Wetenschappen aan de Rijksuniversiteit te Leiden, Leiden.

Jaspars, J. *et al.* (1971). Order effects in impression formation: A psycholinguistic approach. *In* "Social Contexts of Messages". (E. A. Carswell and R. Rommetveit, eds) pp. 109–125. Academic Press, London.

Johnson, N. F. (1965). The psychological reality of phrase structure rules. *Journal of Verbal Learning and Verbal Behavior*, **4**, 469–475.

Johnson-Laird, P. N. (1970). The perception and memory for sentences. *In* "New Horizons in Linguistics". (J. Lyons, ed.) pp. 261–270. Penguin Books, Harmondsworth.

Johnson-Laird, P. N. and Stevenson, R. (1970). Memory for syntax. *Nature*, **227**, p. 412.

Juilland, A. and Roceric, A. (1972). "The Linguistic Concept of Word. Analytic Bibliography". Mouton, The Hague.

Katagiri, A. (1969). Decoding strategies and linguistic form: verbal learning applications. Unpublished manuscript, University of California.

Katz, J. J. and Fodor, J. A. (1963). The structure of a semantic theory. *Language*, **39**, 170–210.

Kintsch, W. (1974). "The Representation of Meaning in Memory". Lawrence Erl-baum Associates, Hillsdale, New Jersey.

Kintsch, W. and Busche, H. (1969). Homophones and synonyms in short-term memory. *Journal of Experimental Psychology*, **80**, 403–407.

Kirk, S. A., McCarthy, J. J. and Kirk, W. D. (1968). Illinois Test of Psycholinguistic Abilities. Revised edition. Manual.

Kolers, P. A. (1973). Some modes of representation. *In* "Communication and Affect, Language and Thought". (P. Pliner, L. Krames and T. Alloway, eds) pp. 21–44. Academic Press, New York.

Krámsky, J. (1969). "The Word as a Linguistic Unit". Mouton, The Hague.

Kusyszyn, I. and Paivio, A. (1966). Transitional probability, word order and noun abstractness in the learning of adjective-noun paired associates. *Journal of Experimental Psychology*, **71**, 800–805.

Kvale, S. (1974a). Permanence and change in memory. I. Reproduction and recognition of visual figures. *Scandinavian Journal of Psychology*, **15**, 33–42.

Kvale, S. (1974b). Permanence and change in memory. II. Reproduction of words in sentences. *Scandinavian Journal of Psychology*, **15**, 139–145.

Kvale, S. (1974c). The temporality of memory. *Journal of Phenomenological Psychology*, **5**, 7–31.

Lambert, W. E. and Paivio, A. (1956). The influence of noun–adjective order on learning. *Canadian Journal of Psychology*, **10**, 9–12.

Larsen, S. F. (1971). The psychological reality of linguistic segments reconsidered. *Scandinavian Journal of Psychology*, **12**, 113–118.

Lashley, K. S. (1951). The problem of serial order in behavior. *In* "Cerebral Mechanisms in Behavior". (L. A. Jeffress, ed.) pp. 112–136. Wiley, New York.

Lenneberg, E. H. (1967). "Biological Foundations of Language". Wiley, New York.

Lotman, J. (1971). Teser til problemet "Konstens plats bland de modellbildande systemen". *In* "Form och Struktur" (K. Aspelin and B. A. Lundberg, eds) pp. 281–299, PANI Norstedts, Stockholm.

Luchins, A. S. (1958). Definitiveness of impression and primacy-recency in communications. *Journal of Social Psychology*, **48**, 275–290.

Luchins, A. S. (1966a). Primacy-recency in impression formation. *In* "The Order of Presentation in Persuasion" (C. J. Hovland, ed.) pp. 33–61. Yale University Print. New Haven, London, 3.print.

Luchins, A. S. (1966b). Attempts to minimize the impact of first impressions. *In* "The order of presentation in persuasion" (C. J. Hovland, ed.) pp. 62–75. Yale University Press, New Haven, London, 3.print.

Lund, F. H. (1925). The psychology of belief. *Journal of Abnormal and Social Psychology*, **20**, 174–196.

Luria, A. R. (1966). "Higher Cortical Functions in Man", Tavistock Publications, London.

Lyons, J. (1970). "Chomsky", Fontana/Collins, London.

Malcolm, N. (1967). Wittgenstein, Ludwig Josef Johann. *In* "The Encyclopedia of Philosophy" (P. Edwards, ed.) Vol. 8, pp. 327–340. The MacMillan Company and The Free Press, New York.

Margulis, S. T., Costanzo, P. R. and Klein, A. L. (1971). Impression change and favorableness of first impression: A study of population and of commitment effects. *Psychonomic Science*, **22**, 318–320.

Martin, J. E. (1969). Semantic determinants of preferred adjective order. *Journal of Verbal Learning and Verbal Behavior*, **8**, 697–704.

Mayo, C. W. and Crockett, W. H. (1964). Cognitive complexity and primacy-recency effects in impression formation. *Journal of Abnormal and Social Psychology*, **68**, 335–338.

McGinnis, J. H. and Oziel, L. J. (1970). Note: Primacy effects in impression formation. *Perceptual and Motor Skills*, **30**, 393–394.

Mehler, J. (1963). Some effects of grammatical transformations on the recall of English sentences. *Journal of Verbal Learning and Verbal Behaviour*, **2**, 346–351.

Merleau-Ponty, M. (1962). "Phenomenology of Perception". Routledge and Kegan Paul, London, The Humanities Press, New York.

Merleau-Ponty, M. (1965). "The Structure of Behavior", Methuen, London.

Miller, G. A. (1956). The magical number seven plus or minus two: some limits on our capacity for information processing. *Psychological Review*, **63**, 81–97.

Miller, G. A. (1962a). Decision units in the perception of speech. *IRE Transactions on Information Theory*, IT-**8**, 81–83.

Miller, G. A. (1962b). Some psychological studies of grammar. *American Psychologists*, **17**, 748–762.

Miller, G. A. (1965). Some preliminaries to psycholinguistics. *American Psychologists*, **20**, 15–20.

Murdock, B. B. Jr. (1962). The serial position effect of free recall. *Journal of Experimental Psychology*, **64**, 482–488.

Neisser, U. (1966). "Cognitive Psychology", Appleton-Century-Crofts, New York.

Noble, C. E. (1952). An analysis of meaning. *Psychological Review*, **59**, 421–430.

Ornstein, R. E. (1969). "On the Experience of Time", Harmondsworth, England, Penguin Books.

Osgood, C. E. (1952). The nature and measurement of meaning. *Psychological Bulletin*, **49**, 197–237.

Osgood, C. E. (1962). Studies on the generality of affective meaning systems. *The American Psychologist*, **17**, 10–18.

Osgood, C. E., Suci, G. J. and Tannenbaum, P. H. (1957). "The Measurement of Meaning", University of Illinois Press. Urbana.

Paivio, A. (1963). Learning of adjective-noun paired associates as a function of adjective-noun word order and noun abstractness. *Canadian Journal of Psychology*, **17**, 370–379.

Paivio, A. (1969). Mental imagery in associative learning and memory. *Psychological Review*, **76**, 241–263.

Peterson, L. R. and Peterson, M. J. (1959). Short-term retention of individual verbal items. *Journal of Experimental Psychology*, **58**, 193–198.

Postman, L. (1968). Short-term memory and incidental learning. *In* "Categories of Human Learning". (A. W. Melton, ed.) pp. 145–201. Academic Press, New York. Fourth Printing.

Postman, L. and Phillips, L. W. (1965). Short-term temporal changes in free recall. *Quarterly Journal of Experimental Psychology*, **17**, 132–138.

Reichling, A. (1935). "Het Woord". Uitgeverij J J.. Berkhout, Nijmegen.

Reichling, A. (1963). Das Problem der Bedeutung in der Sprachwissenschaft. Insbrucker Beiträge zur Kulturwissenschaft, Sonderheft 19. Innsbruck.

Rommetveit, R. (1968). "Words, Meanings and Messages". Academic Press, New York, Universitetsforlaget, Oslo.

Rommetveit, R. (1972a). Language games, deep syntactic structures, and hermeneutic circles. *In* "The Context of Social Psychology: A Critical Assessment". (J. Israel and H. Tajfel, eds) pp. 212–257. Academic Press, London.

Rommetveit, R. (1972b). Deep structure of sentences versus message structure. Some critical remarks on current paradigms, and suggestions of an alternative approach. *Norwegian Journal of Linguistic*, **26**, 3–32.

Rommetveit, R. (1972c). "Språk, Tanke og Kommunikasjon. Ei Innføring i Språkpsykologi og Psykolingvistikk". Universitetsforlaget, Oslo.

Rommetveit, R. (1974). "On Message Structure. A Framework for the Study of Language and Communication". Wiley, London.

Rommetveit, R. *et al.* (1971). Processing of utterances in context. *In* "Social Contexts of Messages". (E. A. Carswell and R. Rommetveit, eds) pp. 29–56. Academic Press, London.

Rommetveit, R. and Strømnes, F. (1965). Determinants of interpretation of homonyms in a word association context. *Pedagogisk Forskning*, **9**, 179–184.

Rommetveit, R. and Turner, E. A. (1967). A study of 'chunking' in transmission of messages. *Lingua*, **18**, 337–351.

Rosenbaum, M. E. and Levin, I. P. (1968). Impression formation as a function of source credibility and order of presentation of contradictory information. *Journal of Personality and Social Psychology*, **10**, 167–174.

Sachs, J. D. S. (1967). Recognition memory for syntactic and semantic aspects of connected discourse. *Perception and Psychophysics*, **2**, 437–442.

Savin, H. B. and Perchonock, E. (1965). Grammatical structure and immediate recall of English sentences. *Journal of Verbal Learning and Verbal Behavior*, **4**, 348–353.

Schlesinger, I. M. (1971). The grammar of sign language and the problem of language universals. *In* "Biological and Social Factors in Psycholinguistics". (J. Morton, ed.) pp. 98–121, Logos, London.

Schulman, H. G. (1971). Similarity effects in short-term memory. *Psychological Bulletin*, **75**, 399–415.

Schulman, H. G. (1972). Semantic confusion errors in short-term memory. *Journal of Verbal Learning and Verbal Behavior*, **11**, 221–227.

Schultink, H. (1962). On word identity. *Lingua*, **11**, 354–362.

Skjerve, J. (1971). Word sequence and recall. *In* "Social Contexts of Messages". (E. A. Carswell and R. Rommetveit, eds) pp. 139–142. Academic Press, London.

Sperling, G. (1960). The information available in brief visual presentations. *Psychological Monographs*, **74**, no. 11.

Stewart, R. H. (1965). Effect of continuous responding on the order effect in personality impression formation. *Journal of Personality and Social Psychology*, **1**, 161–165.

Sutherland, N. S. (1968). Outlines of a theory of visual pattern recognition in animals and man. *Proceedings of the Royal Society, Series 1B*, **171**, 297–317.

Teleman, U. *et al.* (1973). Åtta texter Ar Dagens Nyheter. En läsbarhetsstudie Meddelanden från Avdelingen för tillämpad nordisk språkvetenskap. Institutionen för nordiska pråk. Lunds Universitet. Lund.

Tzeng, O. J. L. (1973). Positive recency effect in delayed free recall. *Journal of Verbal Learning and Verbal Behavior*, **12**, 436–439.

Uhlenbeck, E. M. (1963). An appraisal of transformation theory. *Lingua*, **12**, 1–18.

Uhlenbeck, E. M. (1967). Some further remarks on transformational grammar. *Lingua*, **17**, 263–316.

Ullmann, S. (1957). "The Principles of Semantics". Jackson, Son and Co., Glasgow, Basil Blackwell, Oxford.

Van Mierlo, H. (1968). Challenges for lingustics. *Lingua*, **21**, 535–542.

Van Wyk, E. B. (1968). Notes on word autonomy. *Lingua*, **21**, 543–557.

Vendler, Z. (1963). The grammar of goodness. *The Philosophical Review*, **72**, 446–465.

Waugh, N. C. and Norman, D. A. (1965). Primary memory. *Psychological Review*, **72**, 89–104.

Weinreich, U. (1963). On the semantic structure of language. *In* "Universals of Language". (J. H. Greenberg, ed.) pp. 114–171. The M.I.T. Press, Cambridge, Mass.

Winer, B. J. (1962). "Statistical Principles in Experimental Design". McGraw-Hill, New York.

Yngve, V. H. (1960). A model and a hypothesis for a language structure. *Proceedings of the American Philosophical Society*, **104**, 444–466.

Yuille, J. C., Paivio, A. and Lambert, W. E. (1969). Noun and adjective imagery and order in paired-associate learning by French and English subjects. *Canadian Journal of Psychology*, **23**, 459–466.

Author Index

Subject Index